D1644904

ROLLING DOWN THE LEA

by the same author

I FOLLOW ST. PATRICK

COLLECTED FORMS

OLIVER ST. JOHN GOGARTY

Rolling down the Lea

‘There was the Liffey rolling down the lea’
SPENSER: Faerie Queen

CONSTABLE · LONDON

LONDON
PUBLISHED BY
Constable and Company Ltd
10–12 Orange Street, W.C.2

INDIA
Orient Longmans Ltd
BOMBAY CALCUTTA MADRAS

CANADA
Longmans, Green and Company
TORONTO

SOUTH *and* EAST AFRICA
Longmans Green and Company, Limited
CAPE TOWN NAIROBI

First published . . . 1950

Printed in Great Britain by
RICHARD CLAY AND COMPANY, LTD.
BUNGAY
SUFFOLK

ERRATA

Page v. The Greek quotation should read:

μηκέτι ὑδροπότει, ἀλλ' οἴνω
ὀλίγω χρῶ, διὰ τὸν στόμαχόν σου
καὶ τὰς πυκνάς σου ἀσθενείας

Paul to Timothy

Page 112, line 9. *For* 'Chopin's' *read* 'Schubert's'.

To

T. A. COSTELLO

μηκέτι ὑδοροπότει ἀλλά οἴνῳ ὀλίγῳ χρῶ
δὶα τὸν στόμαχον καὶ τὰς πυκνάς σου
ἀσθενείας

CONTENTS

CHAPTER ONE

‘ No Mean City ’

IRELAND, LIKE ITS fabulous islands in the Western Ocean, is visible only once in seven years. So now is the time to catch a glimpse of it. If you believe airline advertisements, you will imagine that all you have to do is to take your grip and step on board a silver-shining cleaver of the skies to reach Europe from America in the morning. The advertisements do not specify how long it may be between your grip and your step. That is why, to a leisurely soul like mine, air travel appeals more than a trip in an ocean liner or even in a windjammer. It is not necessarily so speedy or so regular.

I have flown the Atlantic off and on since the days when seaplanes took off at Foynes and landed at Port Washington. That was before air-ways became important enough to engage the attention of the ‘ Authorities ’; and, as a result, to be endowed with pomp and spancelled with red tape. That is why some years ago it took two months and eight days before I could get a reservation. And when one came, it was at midnight with a quarter of an hour's notice, and no taxi to the airport five or six miles from Limerick at Rineanna.

I had used all the influence I could bring to bear to obtain a 'priority' by which I was enabled to get a seat in front of the many who were waiting. I got before them, and boarded a twenty-six seater with twenty-three empty seats. Do not think that I am complaining. That is one of the advantages of red tape: it disheartens the unsophisticated and leaves the old stager plenty of room. It also reduces possible casualties: in my case from a possible twenty-six to three. I will admit that the bird-like flutter at the last minute adds a thrill that suggests flying, a thrill that would be absent if you went by sea. Then there is the additional diversion that you never know where you may land. The last time I flew intending New York, I landed in Labrador. The long wait for the priority had conditioned me, so I had plenty of time on hand. I could pity the poor sea-passengers who would be put ashore at the irrevocable hour on schedule without a hope—except an iceberg—of seeing more than they had paid for: out of bounds for them was the silence and spaciousness of Labrador.

Red Tape, and not the serpent, is the cause of the Fall of Man. Eve, even without a mother to prompt her, took a coil of it; and had Adam where she wanted him for the rest of his days. His descendants have never ceased filling out forms.

In the days of the flying-boat you were provided with a bed; but in these modern times all you get is a chair that slopes backwards and suggests a shave or a haircut more than a sleep. Nevertheless, you can land at Shannon safely if the magnetic mountain in the vicinity has not queered the altmeter and brought you down in defiance of all the lines' red tape. But why dribble any farther? Let me shoot at the goal. There will be plenty of time, I can vouch for that, to describe my pleasant journey from the airport to the town. But here we are in the capital of Tín na nóg, the Land of the Ever Young.

Dublin. Dublin of the vistas! What names come to mind, names filling more than two centuries from the days of the gloomy Dean Swift, who left his money to found a lunatic asylum 'to show by one sarcastic touch no nation needed it so much', to Mrs. Bernard Shaw, who left her money to teach manners to Irishmen; and some say (they would in Dublin) that, in spite of all his acumen, the man for whom it was principally intended failed to see the sarcastic touch; Oliver Goldsmith; Bishop Berkeley, who wrote 'Westward the course of Empire takes its way' and went his way to Rhode Island and gave his name to Berkeley, California; Hamilton, who discovered proleptically the Quaternion

Theory by the banks of the Royal Canal; Burke, who thundered in defence of American liberation; Molyneux, whose nationalism caused his books to be burned by the common hangman; Fitzgerald, who anticipated Marconi in the discovery of ætherial waves; Mahaffy, who was the greatest Humanist of his time as well as the expeller from Trinity College of Oscar Wilde to Oxford; down to Yeats, Æ, and lastly James Joyce, in whose *Anna Livia Plurabelle* the whole history of Dublin may be discerned by thought, this time cataleptic. All these men lived in Dublin, but most of them died elsewhere. Dublin, that stick of a rocket which remains on the ground while its stars shoot off to light the darkness and die enskied.

I could see that, over the way in the Green, the chestnuts were pinnacled with countless blossoms. Such a year for flowering Spring! The severest winter in memory must have done good in its secret way, for, though the Spring was cold, the blossoms were profuse and lasting. What a glorious morning! I took a turn to the left along Merrion Row. The One-Eyed Man had changed hands—most taverns do. It is Durkin's now; now it is Sweeney's; now it is Kennedy's. What is it that the old gloss, written a thousand years ago by a monk on the edge of his parchment, said about the fort of Rathangan? It had many captains.

'It was Aed's, it was Ailill's,
It was Conaing's, it was Cuiline's;
The fort remains after each man in his turn—
And the kings asleep in the ground.'

'And the kings asleep in the ground.' The fort remains after each man in his turn. So it is with the Dublin taverns; but the change is quicker.

A café stood next to a locked gate, over which was an inscription cut in stone 'Huguenot Cemetery 1693'. I looked through the railings which protected it from the street. Within were a few oblong stones raised on four square pillars. The inscriptions were faded; but not so the lilacs which were holding their funeral torches over the dead. The gold of the laburnums was still to spend. It was 'in reserve', as became men who founded banks in the city that gave them sanctuary.

The best of Dublin was built between 1750 and 1800. After that the blight of Union, that Union which acted like a vacuum-cleaner and sucked everything into itself; but, unlike that machine, left vacuum behind. For more than a century Dublin was sucked dry to the tune of 'good form'; but the stately houses remain to show the grandeur that has departed. They are tenements, some of them, some of them are Government offices which lack the glamour of tenement life; but the rose-red shadows they cast in the twilight bring back the purple splendour of the prime.

The city of about half a million people is divided by the River Liffey, which is only fifty yards wide at its largest bridge. It should have been called the City of the Seven Bridges; but in the days such places were given names it had but a ford of hurdles and no bridge.

It is one of the most beautiful cities in Europe, with its five squares, its domes and the Palladian architecture of its public edifices.

The names of the squares and the streets record its history, which is the history of the English Lords Lieutenants or of the soldiers who held the country for their kings and queens. Rutland Square, where the Duke of Ormonde had his town house; Mountjoy Square, commemorating the good soldier who drove Don Juan d'Aquila back to Spain and to a court martial on the conduct of his invasion of Kinsale; Fitzwilliam Square—the descendant of that good Earl is still alive—Merrion Square, where the famous doctors lived from whose presence it got its nickname, 'The Valley of the Shadow of Death'. Here in No. 1 dwelt Sir William Wilde, the father of Oscar, a man of inordinate appetites famous in his own right: no mastoid operation can begin without the incision called after Wilde. In this first of the houses on the north side of the square also lived 'Speranza', the mother of Oscar, who had her drawing-rooms darkened and joss-sticks burned at three o'clock in the afternoon. On the south side, within a door of one another, lived the poets, Yeats and Æ, who went to call on each other at the same time; Yeats passed with his head in the air, Æ passed with his head sunk in his beard, resolving many mysteries. On calling, each was told that the other was out.

About one third of the way along the vista of rose-red confronting the greenery of the square, the customary granite steps are replaced by ostentatious steps of white marble. This was the house of the famous sporting surgeon, Johnny MacCardle, who may have missed a patient or two, but never missed a race-meeting. At one of these a jockey fell and broke his neck. Instinctively the crowd turned to the grand stand. They were right. The surgeon was there, but not exposed to the cold of the seats so much as to that of the ice surrounding the Heidseick. His acolytes took him by the Persian-lamb lapels and led him out protesting that there was no such thing as an urgent accident. He knelt down and found that the jockey's neck was a grating universal joint. He arose. Silence for the pronunciamento—‘ Boys, he's dead; but I'll do all I can.’ Doctors say that ‘ where there's life there's hope ’; but here we are trespassing on the mysteries.

Aside, to the right before the long vista begins, is the great mansion where the Duke of Wellington, Blucher's protégé, was nursed. He was born in a coach on the way to Dublin. Hence, perhaps, his remark that ' to be born in a stable does not make you a horse '. He should have said ' " Coach " does not make you a postilion '.

The long vista is closed to the east by a strange church. It stands in Mount Street Crescent; and its steeple consists of copies of two well-known architectural features superimposed: one called the Lanthorn of Diogenes, the other the Temple of the Winds. The latter may have questionable appropriateness to a church; but so intent was the XVIIIth century on steeples that it was thought that no church could be complete without one, and this even though the main edifice was modelled on a Greek temple of the classical or pagan period. It took Dean Swift much of his caustic denunciation to prevent a brick spire from being stuck on the tower of Comyn's fine cathedral. Alas, the outrage was canonised and committed. Needless to say, this after the death of the pungent Dean.

Every man in Ireland is a ' character ', that is to say that he has a soul of his own and expresses it individually; if words fail him, by actions. In Dublin some of these characters preserve their own self-respect or vanity, by veiling their malevolence in an assumption of friendliness. Malevolence is their nearest approach to superiority. Dublin, as Yeats called it, is a ' bitter ' town. However, I was born there, and I am—who knows?—maybe somewhat astringent, so, when my sharp-nosed acquaintance hailed me with, 'Your book is banned. The Censors have banned it,' he could not suppress his glee.

'Naturally,' I said. And he was taken aback. 'Which one?' I then asked casually.

'*Mr. Petunia*.' He had it pat.

'That's rather exasperating,' I said, as if I cared.

His interest rose.

'That's a nuisance,' I continued. 'I wish the Censors had timed it better, waited a month or so.'

He was all agog. So I *was* put out by his news.

'Why did you want them to wait a month?'

'It's a long recital,' I began. I hoped that he would carry away even half of what I was about to say; but I knew that he couldn't hold anything that had the least trace of subtlety in it; but I let him have it for whomever would get the garbled version.

'Try to remember this. When I voted for the Censor Bill, I did so eagerly because I realised that, during the periods that censorship was most astringent, literature was most remarkable. The Inquisition produced some of the greatest geniuses of Europe. And in England, in Oxford, the Martyrs' Memorial commemorates the golden years of English prose. And it is on the style of English prose that an Englishman relies for his salvation. If the Bible came to him through French, he would be damned beyond redemption; but it came to him literally illuminated by its translators.

'There was some heat in controversy in those days. Only for the king and the clemency of Pope Clement VII, Rabelais would have been burned at the stake for the matter of a comma; but he talked over the heads of the censors who would make anyone think that they were chosen as a rule for their ignorance of literature and their sensitiveness to the stimuli of lascivious suggestions. That is why the censors are always either old or celibate, or both, which make a vigilant censor. While they are nosing out smut, the author, if he is worth his salt, is getting by them with literature. It would seem, from a survey of the history of censorship, that censors were appointed as "interference" (a phrase from American football) to hold off the empty man while the player in possession gets by.

'With this in mind, I voted for as many censors as the Church and State thought fit to appoint. I knew that they would not interfere with good literature or deprive the nation of any writing that was thoughtful, spermatic and edifying.

'What was the result? I myself was one of the first to be banned. Little did I imagine that sex obsession would be more alluring than style.'

'Your books could not have been that way,' he

interjected, only half understanding the argument. A thought made him vague.

'A moment,' I said. 'Don't interrupt your Stream of Consciousness. Now, as I could not consider that my lucubrations were in the tradition of great literature, literature that would be above the capacity of paltry people as the poems of the ollaves of old were above the heads of the uninitiated, I refused to submit my books to capricious censorship. Note: "capricious" means being like a he-goat.'

He began to wriggle. Reasoning made him restless.

'Hold it for a minute,' I entreated. Then, to arouse his curiosity, 'Don't you see what this means?'

He examined the question as a hen examines a speck of meal. 'It means,' I said with all the emphasis I could summon, 'that censors will have to send outside for their smut as a fishwife with a hang-over sends out for a pint of porter in the morning.'

Inarticulate sounds of inattention told me that I was talking to an intermittent mind.

'Must I go on talking to myself, as the modern writers do? I said that to have my book banned at this juncture was exasperating. Do you know why? Because I was employing all the influences I could direct to have it banned in Boston. Now, that would be worth while, for any book that is banned in Boston is boomed in the rest of the United States. But, just as some friends of mine were trying to make the Boston booksellers believe that my book, which is a study in psychiatry—I am referring to *Mr. Petunia*—was at root pornographical, over comes word that it has been banned in Dublin. In Dublin, where they banned *Old Moore's Almanac!* with its harmless prognostications. That was enough for the Bostonians. They thought—don't you see?—that my book was about things that cast their shadows before: brassières and the like. How could the Boston censors stoop to that? It was most disconcerting. I, who had expected thunder, heard only a fiske. Instead of protecting works of genius, Irish censors are only protecting (commercially) religious pamphlets. I don't want to be banned in Dublin again. No one asks a eunuch for an opinion on divorce.

'Prudery and stupidity have been problems in every civilisation. All poets have been confronted by both. Censors.' I endorsed myself by a quotation from that blameless man, Gerald Griffin:

> 'Had bounteous Nature's counsel hung
> Upon your will severe,
> Tom Moore had ne'er green Erin sung;
> Nor Burns the Banks of Ayr.'

With what pity do we regard the old-maidish men who called Shakespeare 'Smutster and punster'.

'Brakki kekkax koax koax! If Aristophanes tried to get his "Clouds" played in Dublin! Holy smoke!'

He was gone like a cloud from the Moetic Lake.

The sun was shining. People were smiling. They were all well dressed. The faces of the girls were as gay as their costumes. Visitors were everywhere. Prices were higher than ever before, but there was money to pay them. There was not a shop or a store to be rented. Houses cost six or seven, aye up to ten, times more than they cost a few years ago. And this in spite of the fact that the city's taxes were 125 per cent. Englishmen were as plentiful as rabbits. After all, there must be some magic in Sean T.'s hat, I remarked to myself as I leaned on the parapet of Dublin Bridge, looking west. 'There was the Liffey rolling down the lea', changed from the days when the poet Spenser saw it, because it is now contained by walls on each side. But it is still rolling down the lea.

Geologists tell us that there was time when the Liffey did not roll down the lea at all, but rushed for Dublin Bay as directly as the River Dodder does. That was before the Liffey burst its banks at Poulaphoca to go meandering for sixty miles or so through the rich plains of Kildare, mirroring horses and trees in its black, still reaches, and tempting salmon fresh from the sea with little cascades, until, after its last fall at Leixlip, which is the name the Viking pirates who founded Dublin gave to the Salmon Leap, it took the tide where Iseult's chapel once stood, and rolled down the lea.

Today on both sides of the river the lea is covered with the most perfect examples of Georgian architecture that remain, now that a great part of London is demolished or replaced. Dublin stands about its river very much as when the City Fathers planned it at the end of the XVIIIth century. True, its principal street is vulgar and bizarre, with plaster palaces and neon lights that make the day tawdry and the night hideous; but in its guarded squares, uncrowded streets and quiet culs-de-sac and along the canals, a loveliness still lingers from a century that is gone. Among rose-red houses, public buildings of white stone rise, crowned with various domes of copper, green with age.

The pillared Custom House is reflected in the water when the river is brimful at high tide. They say that the architect of the Four Courts died of a broken heart because his plans for such another water-reflected pile were rejected.

It is well for him that he did not live to see stucco in the broadest street of the city or turf in the great park.

But I have promised to reiterate my trip to Dublin from Shannon port.

It is not my fault that the tale begins tangentially, and so is somewhat abrupt. But it was abrupter to me because I was watching the large gold pieces that the sun was squandering under the trees that met over the road, and I was thinking that the woodbine would be already open on another planet, provided of course that it grew there.

CHAPTER TWO

'What durst you, Sir?'

'HAVE YOU EVER heard tell of What's That, the quean of Cootehill?'

Spring comes to Ireland gradually and lingers through all May and well into June. No petal falls from the chestnut pinnacles while lilac and laburnum bloom. The lilac waits for the laburnum to blossom, and they are still blossoming when the hawthorn whitens fragrantly and fills the tranquil air about it with heady balm.

They tell me that Winter here was colder than any Winter within living memory: man and beast died of cold; floods carried off the hayricks and laid waste the fields. There was great scarcity of fuel, and what turf there was, was damp. Even the long and lovely Spring could not make people forget the hardship they had endured. I wondered if the severe Winter was the cause of the unusually bounteous Spring, for, like many another, I find myself casting about for cause and effect. In this instance the old, deep-seated idea of compensation was at work. And I might have gone on following this dialectic had not the question stated above begun to intrude into what reviewers nowadays are pleased to call 'the Stream of Consciousness', which would appear to be a stream with no banks, in which modern novelists flounder in default of a current or an estuary. Incoherence is explained by 'Subjectivity'. In other words, the author is himself the subject.

Far be it from me to present myself as my own subject. I take very little credit for being conscious.

Where hedges rose, they were bright and black. I was in no mood to particularise. I wished to become a part of the genial scene.

Be this as it may, let me state here that I resented being asked if I had ever heard tell of What's That, not because it might have interrupted and disturbed my contemplation of the season's golden pomp (though of course it might have fitted nicely into my Stream of Consciousness), but because, though meant in all friendliness, it was over familiar, and therefore impertinent in its way. Of that I have no doubt, for unless such a question is asked by an old friend, it obtrudes on a man's dignity, implying as it did that he is interested in the *demi-monde*. And a friend would have to be a very old friend indeed to ask me such a question. Only my besetting sin, which is, strangely enough, curiosity, could have made me tolerate such an intrusion and a taking-for-granted that I could possibly be interested. He is making me pay by his familiarity for giving me this lift to town. This is why, instead of saying 'I have not the slightest interest in What's That,' all I said was 'No.'

This led to an explanation which, in turn, led me unaware into a defence of the hoyting girl of Cootehill.

I can well understand why she was wont to ask the question from which she got her nickname among the lewder merchants and the surreptitious bank clerks of Cootehill. Being alone, it became incumbent on her to assume a maidenly unsophistication, and this, as the citizens should have seen, redounded as much to Cootehill's credit as to hers. In fact, had she for a moment permitted herself to become *blasé*, it would have reflected upon the township and brought it into disrepute, because it would have revealed the fact that Cootehill could support but one facile Venus, and that, as a result of the town's illiberality, she had become sophisticated, shameless and over-worked. But by exclaiming 'What's that?' she gave an impression of perennial innocence even though she had it not.

I could have quoted Herrick about a girl who 'is not for one but every night a bride', recurrently fresh; but I felt that it would have been lost on my interrogator. Instead, I defended Modesty in the abstract:

'There's a lot to be said for What's That,' I continued, 'for, by pretending to be innocent, she not only flattered each bank clerk, auctioneer and cattle-dealer by leaving him under the impression that he was the first to gain her favour; but she engendered in him a certain gentleness in love, for who would be so gross as to take advantage of a poor innocent without some "sweet, reluctant, amorous delay", as the Puritan poet has it? Think of the opposite. Would you have her shameless? There is nothing so revolting and demoralising as an immodest woman. Even the pagans of old felt this when they elevated Modestia to a divinity. Would you have her as devil-may-care as good old Mary Anne?'

'Good old Mary Anne?'

'Now, Stephen, don't pretend that you never heard of Mary Anne. She was or is a "roaring girle" of Dublin who, as the song made in her honour—well, not exactly in her honour, but about her—says, "She doesn't care a damn". Picture to yourself the effect of anyone not caring a damn in ethical Cootehill. Why, not only her name, but the names of all her paramours would be all over the town. The whole economic system of Cootehill would be dislocated. For instance, who would deal with a bank in that hamlet of righteousness if one or more of its officials were known to be given to chambering and wantonness? It could be overlooked but not forgotten in, shall we say? the case of an auctioneer who might be "going, going, gone", for all Cootehill would care; but a bank depends on stability, and stability in the last analysis depends on character, and character . . .'

'Wait till you hear what happened.'

'What?' I asked, weakly allowing myself to be diverted from the moral of my homily.

'She struck.'

'Whom?'

'Nobody. But she struck work because they called her What's That. And it served them damn well right. Talk of dislocation! You should have seen Cootehill. It was desperate: those who could not get to Dublin for week-ends applied for a transfer. One banker who was a bachelor resigned.'

Well might she exclaim, I thought:

> 'How many of our sex by such as these
> Have their good thoughts paid with a blasted name
> That never deserved loosely.'

And into my Stream of Consciousness came an old Greek play on how the women of Athens flouted all the men until they should give up their squabbles with another Greek State, and the stringency that ensued. The very thing that What's That did to Cootehill. What a play could be made of that for the Gate Theatre! It's too good for the Abbey. Anyway, in the Abbey it would have to be in Irish, and if you have a smattering of the language and an ignorance of history you may believe that there never was a gay woman in Ireland—that is, if you read history under proper direction. This pious hallucination will hold as long as the Irish are ignorant of their own history. If they had only an inkling of it, Grania would be black-balled for the Cumann na Mbyhan, which more or less corresponds loosely with the Daughters of the Revolution in America.

'One fellow made a kind of sneaking apology; and, dammit, what do you think happened? You could never guess.'

'I could. She accepted it,' I said.

'Accepted! She married him!'

Fresh and fair were the gems she wore.

'Now you see the virtue of modesty.'

'Are you codding?' was all my thanks.

'No, I'm not,' I said; 'for this is no subject for *blague*.'

Not only did her innocence implied in the question from which she got her name bring What's That a husband; but it kept sweet the good name of Cootehill.

Now, there are many Protestants in Cootehill. Protestantism is primarily a regulator of conduct more than a religion. It lays stress on the outer life.

There are many Orangemen, too, in Cootehill; and you know how those rugged and illiberal men refused to yield an inch of their artificial Ulster and their slogan, 'Not an inch'. Therefore, What's That may be considered, with her abnegation, an embodiment of the Orange North. 'Not an inch.'

While good old Mary Anne, with all her liberality and large discourse and 'There's a belly that never bore a bastard', becomes a worthy symbol of the South. Our problem, or rather, the politicians' problem, resolves itself into a merger of What's That with Mary Anne, North with South. Intangibility on the one part; illimitable invitation on the other. 'Not an inch' with 'Let them all come!'

'Wouldn't it settle things quicker if all the women were to take example by What's That and go on a local strike? Then the Orangemen could get a woman only in the South; and *vice versa*, which is Reciprocity, this would bring in the North.'

For a fellow of Stephen's type—that is, a fellow who is a bad listener—his suggestion was admirable. Why had I not thought of it? It showed at least that he had not missed the good intention and the trend of my remarks.

With my mind's eye already I could see troops of sex-starved Orangemen crossing the Border with drums beating and fifes askirl, migrating south to where the only complaisant women were.

Soon my mind outsoared any thought of carnality, and dwelt only on the great cultural influence our Mary Annes would have on the Men of Ulster, and of the sweet reasonableness they would engender in those dour and resolute breasts. The Ulster dames and damoiselles might co-operate in the great Union. I know that it is an opinion heretical in the South; but I cannot help but hold it—The women of the North are better looking than their Southern sisters. I began to think that the plan was not so preposterous as it sounded. One factor, a compelling one, was overlooked: the thought of the return of their terse and take-it-for-granted spouses and lovers would be enough to make the Northern ladies lenient and disposed to try any novelty; and what greater novelty could they find than the woman-shy swains of the South, the sootherers, the blarneyers, the palaverers, the playboys, the jongleurs? There was always the chance that they would take so long in their adulations that the ladies might be driven in desperation to ask them to be more practical and less poetic; and to do something pat. Unless the thought of the fast-working men of Ulster, with their technique of summary coercion let loose among their Southern sweethearts, might act as a spur to the men of the South philandering in Ulster. Who can say that to the Southern ladies it might not come as a great relief?

Meanwhile, the Dovetails and other liberal societies advancing in open order with banners flying gallantly—whereon is displayed a dove with wings addorsed and rising tail—to the Border with bagpipes playing many a ditty of loneliness and love-longing such as

'Saw ye my wee thing? Saw ye my ain thing?'

in dialect as a compliment to the North, would lead the Army in open order to dally with the disdainful maids and matrons of the North in an endeavour to convince them that Popery is no insurmountable obstacle to Union. What good is woman's franchise if she does not use it to unite opposites?

'Why open order?' Stephen asked.

'To facilitate infiltration,' I answered shortly, for I dislike being interrupted in a rhapsody. 'You would not have them serenading in mass formation?' I asked.

He thought that it would be unseemly to send an army against women, however obdurate.

'Not if they sang the National Anthem, "Neutrals are we"'.

'Or "The Cock o' the North",' said Stephen.

If it fails in real life, it can be played in the Abbey Theatre.

A castle covered with Virginia creeper rose on our right. Woods spread not far away. They reminded me of a remark the Earl of Mayo made when we drove one morning to see the hydro-electric works that were being built on the Shannon. Every time we passed a grove of trees he would exclaim, 'Ha! They have not got rid of all the gentlemen yet!'

By which he meant to convey, not snobbishness, but the fact that only the owners of mansions had the sense to know that if you destroyed a country's woods, you exposed the soil to winds, floods and erosion. An ignorant farmer is not his country's pride, but its suicide.

I well remember that trip to inspect the Shannon works. We started off so early in the morning that we arrived in Limerick too early for lunch. We kicked our heels till noon. In Cruise's hotel we lunched at a table covered with smilax. The Earl had been recognised. After lunch we drove to the office of the Shannon Scheme. It was a large yard entered by an arched gateway. No one was about. After much blowing of the horn, followed by shrieks of the siren, a lame man wandered out.

'I have come from Mr. McGilligan to see the Shannon Works,' the Earl announced.

'Mr. McGilligan is out,' the man replied, standing to attention as he did so. He sensed the aristocrat in my companion.

'Of course he is. I left him in Dublin.'

'But this is his brother, Sir, and he's out at lunch.'

The Earl thought a moment, then he turned to me laughing.

'Well, as Lord French says, "What's the use of being Commander-in-Chief if you can't appoint your own staff?"'

His voice changed as we drove off with our permit.

'That lame chap is a good fellow. He served in the last war. That's where he got his wound.'

I didn't know where Lord Mayo got his information; but it and subsequent observations redounded to the credit of McGilligan's Shannon Scheme.

'Whose place is that? I used to know,' I asked Stephen as I pointed to the well-kept castle on the right covered with creepers and crowned by crenellated parapets. But Stephen did not know.

'Where are we?' I asked.

'We're in Roscrea. There's a Trappist monastery here. If you knew more about it you would be less interested in that castle.'

True enough! I might not be interested in anything of this world; but just to show him how far my knowledge of things religious went, I inquired if he were ever a guest of the monks of Roscrea.

'Were you?' he countered.

'Indeed I was.'

'And what did you bring out of it?' he asked, as surprised as he was satirical.

'I got this from a window-pane in the old house.

It was cut with a diamond by the original owner of the place.' I recited,

> 'Mutton is mutton;
> Pork is pork,
> And both are good to eat.
> Ham is ham
> And lamb is lamb;
> But only beef is MEAT.'

The writer must have felt this so intensely that the power of his spiritual mood, as Æ would say, attracted its opposite in a community of vegetarians. In fact it took many Carthusians to deliver his spirit from the flesh.

Strange! The moment I mentioned 'Carthusians' the name of the owner of the pleasantly seated castle occurred to me.

'Colonel Charteris!' I exclaimed. 'We must be in Cahir.' Another contrast. 'He gives shooting parties. At one of them the Marquess of Headfort dropped dead. He was a Senator with the Earl of Mayo in my time.'

My companion winced, but his car did not swerve.

'Dropped dead?' he asked.

I could see that he could not appreciate tragedy. To induce the calm which it should bring, I said, 'It's merely a matter of propinquity. Now, on the planet Neptune, where a day is as long as five of our months, and all our banks would go out of business, the Marquess would not have dropped dead, but subsided gradually, fortified (if we had inter-planetary communication) leisurely by the rites of whatever church claimed him. It's what they call Relativity now; but when I was at school we called it the third law of Kepler. Nobody then thought of broadcasting as a new discovery, something enunciated three hundred and thirty years ago. Indeed, it would have been impracticable then, for there was no semi-sophisticated public nor channels of publicity. So doth Slow Motion take the sting from death. . . .'

He tried to think it out. He was hoping for a place where no one could drop dead, but he was of the earth, earthy.

'I ought to be driving you back to the Abbey of Roscrea,' he said at length. His mind was still associated with death.

An empty cart approached, swaying on the rutted road. The driver tipped his cap. Then he leapt from his newly painted cart, which cheered the eye with its brightly painted reds and blues.

'Could I be lendin' you a hand?' he asked. It was his way of hiding his curiosity. 'Ye haven't run out of gasoline?'

Now, if Stephen would only gas himself and pass out for ten minutes, I might have an interesting talk with this native of the district. But what to me would be an interesting talk might not have seemed so to Stephen; and he would have interrupted.

His manners lack reserve. Of this the reader has become painfully aware from the very first sentence with which this chapter opens. For this reason, and not for any lack of humanity in me, did I wish that he would pass out painlessly while I chatted with the carter. But such a stage of subterfuge was unnecessary.

The man turned to me after eyeing my grey felt hat.

'I would take you for a stranger in these parts?'

The thought shot through my mind: If he finds out that I am a native, I'll learn nothing. So I said, 'I hear that somewhere round here is the most horribly haunted house in the world.'

He eyed me suspiciously. After an anxious pause during which his eye never faltered, 'That would be Leap Castle,' he said, and pronounced it 'Lep'.

Now, Leap Castle is probably first on the books of the society that deals with haunted houses in the British Isles. I had heard much about Leap Castle from many friends. Some had been visitors to it, guests of the family called Derby, to whom it had passed. And Yeats, who loved such things, had more than once discussed with me the elemental that haunted it. This materialised in the form of a large black ram with a thick fleece. It had the face of a decomposing human head. When it appeared, the stench was overpowering. In spite of this Yeats affirmed that it was not an evil spirit. He may have said that it was not an 'elemental'! I am unfamiliar with the terms spiritualists apply to the different unearthly visitants. I remember that when he talked about it, his voice was grave and authoritative. I need not go into the various adventures of those who saw the ghost, nor associate the hauntings with the skeletons in armour that were found immured in the castle walls because in those days when a member of the garrison was killed during a siege his body was walled up. The besiegers were not to be counted on to give him decent burial.

There was a silence, during which his scrutiny continued. At length, 'It was burned down during the Troubles.'

I took care not to jump to the conclusion that it was burned down by the Black and Tans, irresponsible guerillas or gorillas loosed upon Ireland by Lloyd George. The places they burned were not as a rule homes of the gentry. Mansions were burned by the I.R.A. because they might be occupied by the Black and Tans—so the explanation—but really because they belonged to men of English stock. But the underlying cause, I do not fear to affirm it, was the spirit of destruction inherent in the masses which is loosed whenever law and order are in abeyance. It would appear to arise from an inborn hatred in the unworthy for all that leisure and graceful living can produce. One need not go to Russia for examples. It is universal once the reins drop.

'So that is the end of it?'

He became secretive, almost furtive. But he did not wish so old and famous a castle to be summarily dismissed.

'There's nights when it goes on fire.'

I saw the empty windows filled with a red glow. I knew enough. That which haunted it was still there. Few spots on earth are favourable to ghostly presences, and they are reluctant to abandon those.

'I came to drive you from the airport, and not to have you talking about the ghost of Roscrea,' Stephen interposed.

'What else is there to talk about in Ireland except ghosts, from Finn mac Cool to Michael Collins? All ghosts. There is never a good word to be said for the living in this country. It is not until they become ghosts that calumny ceases. That is why I prefer ghost stories to speeches'; but I held my whist.

'Come on! Jump in!'

Misassociation has so often been my lot in life that I have become almost used to it. I jumped in.

I waved to the man with the red cart as we steered for Dublin. Had I said 'Cheerio', it would have been incongruous, as incongruous as J. J. Walsh when, in the middle of the epidemic of Gaelic revival, walking silk-hatted down the quays of Cork, he answered a fishwife's greeting, 'Laun braw' with 'Law braw, by Jove!'

We drove down the straight of the Phoenix Park. It is over two miles long, and it formed the finish for motor races years ago. Now it is like passing between dark walls. On either side, shutting out one of the pleasantest views on earth, long-drawn-out pyramids of melting turf were stacked mile after mile by de Valera's administrators.

'Gracious!' I exclaimed. 'Look what has happened to the finest Park in Europe. Was there no place else to disfigure than the Park?' I remembered what I was thinking about paltry people. 'It all goes back to housing,' I said.

'Housing?' Stephen inquired, puzzled.

'Maybe I was too quick. Let me explain. Those born in slums have a slum outlook. They have been deprived of beauty. They have become tolerant of dirt. And this is the result. They cannot comprehend what they are destroying. But if they thought for a moment about other people, they would not ruin what does not belong to them. This Park is a national possession; it is not owned by a gang that governs or misgoverns the country for a while. The Park is not a wood-pile or a turf-stack.'

I said no more because I was downcast with the thought that the people cannot or (what is worse) do not protest. They permit the slum-minded when in office to spread slumdom over everything that is fine and fair, mental and physical. How long, O Lord, how long, until we have an election to rid us of 'Dev.'?

I thanked him again for his great kindness in coming so far out of his way to drive me across country. He was one of the few good fellows who are unaccountably kind. I dwelt upon his kindness with gratitude, but his opening question still rankled a little in my mind because of its idiom, 'Have you ever heard tell?' Why couldn't he have said, 'Have you heard?' By using a tense which was a kind of past imperfect he suggested existence over a period of time, making What's That, as it were, a thing of the past, whereas she was alive, espoused and flourishing. It made me see, too, that his was the idiom I should have to adopt while living in a country of which I have ever heard tell.

CHAPTER THREE

'This Mortal Coil'

'BECAUSE HE'S A huer and a bastard!'

I had just left the haunt of ancient peace only to walk into MacGlornan. It is amazing what you may find once you come out through the wicket in the Front Gate. Trinity College was behind me, with its smooth lawns, its sleeping Dons and its golden memories. Talking of things golden, I had just left Richard Best in the College Park. He was walking from the Library, probably. He was in a hurry, so he asked me to come to his house any evening to continue our talk. Richard Best, the scholar. I remembered how, years ago, he confided to me that there was only one alternative: religion or scholarship. And I remembered, too, how George Moore had described his golden hair and his unageing, pink complexion, described him as one envious, for Moore's own hair that had been red once was yowden now.

'But I asked you a simple question. I did not mean to offend you,' I continued soothingly to Mac.

Over his tightly buttoned, thin raincoat, the broad, honest, yet fox-like face, with its high, hectic cheek-bones, stared at me with gleaming eyes.

'I had a job all right till he found out that I was a Stater.'

'Well, well,' I said sympathetically, while I tried to get the connection.

MacGlornan was an honest, earnest fellow in spite of the fact that he was a professional politician of the lighter sort. A 'ward-heeler' he would be called in the U.S.A. I realised that he had just lost some appointment that had been promised to him because, on looking into his dossier, somebody had dug up the fact that he had worked at election time for the Government previously in power. As if such a thing mattered; but in the precarious profession of politics such conduct was unforgivable So here he was, hungry, out of a job, a family to provide for and no prospect where every 'Organiser' had been already appointed. No wonder he became excited when I witlessly asked him, 'What are you doing now?'

'Let me tell you that bastard goes into everything before he'll let a blind man get a job breaking stones.'

His mood changed suddenly. He felt that I was too remote from his affairs to be enlistened.

'Ah, to hell with it!' he exclaimed, impatient of

unpleasantness, as all Irishmen are. 'Let's go somewhere and have a quick one.'

I regretted persuasively that I could not go. Even with the whole morning before me, I had no time for 'a quick one'. Politics had not as yet sunk sufficiently deep into my subconscious stream.

'Jaysus!' he exclaimed. 'Trinity College must have ruined you. They lock themselves up like the Friendly Brothers when they are drinking there.'

'Friendly Brothers,' I repeated. 'I have just met two of them, law-abiding citizens on their way to 42 St. Stephen's Green.'

'Law-abiding! I should think they are. Those fellows came over here after, oh, bloody well after the Battle of the Boyne, to see what they could pick up; and they have formed themselves into a club to dodge danger. Friendly, me neck! They were raised on celery.'

Behind me, the Dons dreamed on. The politics of Cleon, innocuous now, and the decline of Athens were their concern. They could study as in a microcosm what had happened, and from that still life deduce what is bound to happen again. Humanity is human at every phase of its history; and Athens provides a pattern and presents us with a formula for all time. World politics is only Athens to the *n*th. Meanness, chicanery and self-interest, all were there. So clearly cut is the statue that we have ceased to analyse the substance. With this in mind, I grew tolerant, for what confronted me in the person of MacGlornan was but politics in action and very much alive. It would be an easy thing to scorn had it not been a part of life, or of whatever vitality Dublin can lend life. Athens was all life. The minds of its citizens had less restricted curiosity and were suppler. The climate helped them with its most pellucid air. The difference between us is only one of degree of dampness. You must not blame Irish politics for not being as corrupt as Athenian politics: vanity, envy, deception, self-justification, endless expatiation, nepotism, honesty, courage, altruism, patriotism—all are here. The pace is slower; and they lack the magical mist of Time and an able panegyrist to make them classical and even edifying. I have never been afraid of Life such as it is. Why should I be now? The fact is I want a man of greater calibre than MacGlornan and more independent, to praise, denounce and project the situation so that I may get it into some perspective. I will wait until I come across one who is above the petty and immediate concerns of politics, an observer unmoved and serene.

I walked across what had once been College Green, upstream against the flood of oratory that was pouring out of Grattan's bronze mouth, too full for sound. Atkinson's poplin shop was to the left, and near it the National Bank, which hides in one of its vestibules Andrew O'Connor's magnificent statue of another orator whose words were, like Henry Grattan's, cast in bronze. The pillared Parliament House was on the right; its 'ironic' columns, as Joyce would say, held the Bank of Ireland now. Shelley commented on this when he came to Dublin at the beginning of the last century, so it would be presumptuous of me to comment on it now. I will only remark that the sounds therein of the adding-machines are dispassionate; and, if inarticulate, exact.

How pink and white are the complexions of the people! MacGlornan was like an apple. The girls looking into Atkinson's window are like Dresden shepherdesses—pinker than ever now by contrast, since the town is becoming more and more brunetted by hordes of dark, hard-eyed little men and fat, blowzy women, self-displaced from England for the flesh-pots of the capital of a food-producing country.

I am very careful to refrain from saying that Ireland is a strange country, just as I have come to deny myself comment on the shapes seen in a restaurant, for I never forget that I am part of the show. This Bernard Shaw overlooked when, after reading Joyce, he exclaimed, 'If such characters really exist, there should be a commission to enquire, Why?' He should have been prepared for them. He was born in Dublin. He spent his youth in it. He was part of the show himself. But he left it as soon as possible, you will object. That matters not. Dean Swift was born in Dublin. As Shaw himself says, ‘ That was enough.’ He, too, was part of the show.

Here is a lady pink and white. Before me stands Dulcie. Her eyes are of that blue that is neither light blue nor violet, and yet not one blue, but two blues that are often melted into one, around large pupils. Now these pupils were all but level with my own.

She stood before me smiling, and never said a word. She watched my eyes, waiting for recognition to dawn. Thank God she did not say ‘ You don't know me.’ She was anything but banal. I waited, too, as I gazed at her neck with its poreless Irish skin. Then up came the memory of Robin. I remembered his explanation, ‘ It's more matey,’ for sleeping in such a narrow bed. And this is Dulcie. How sweetly she smiled! Nothing inscrutable about it: the smile of a companionable woman.

I said, ‘ It's you that is looking well.’

She made a joke and smiled. I caught the glimpse of even teeth.

I said, ‘ You have not altered. What are you doing? Where are you living now? Are you real or some personification of Ireland? ’

She shook her head.

'And you have not forgotten Robin?'

'Could I ever forget him? Those were the days.'

She smiled regretfully, for the days when there was nothing bounded by any ring.

I marvelled at the power Robin had over women. He was 'rantin', rovin'', if ever a lad was. Bald and by no means good-looking, yet he was prepossessing. Maybe his dark eyes and his deep voice mesmerised them, and the way he had of taking the harm out of things by taking everything for granted. How Dulcie regretted him! Her eyes deepened. She was near to tears. I rallied her to cheer up:

'What a fine figure! Your regular features and your silken skin. You can pick and choose, though, as a rule; the lovelier the woman the more worthless the man she marries.'

'That won't be the way with me,' she said.

'Will you ever forget the trailer?' I asked.

She forgot to look embarrassed, but smiled gaily.

'You are asking *me*,' she answered and pointed to herself.

I went on, trying to give an imitation of Robin as he joined his friends at the bibbery asking in his deep voice:

'Will none of you blighters ever laugh?'

'He never gave himself a chance,' she said.

On this we agreed, nodding knowingly. She shook hands and went her way, leaving me with memories that were sad and glad. Sad, because Robin was gone, though it was just in time before infirmity caught up with him; and glad that Dulcie was happy and still fancy free.

What is about to be said now used to be said only of the Saints. Dulcie, when I knew her, had not been classified in that category. And yet she has one characteristic of the Saints, that is, of some of them: she has fragrance. Now, I hate perfumes as much as Flaccus did. Dulcie has no need for them. She has a fragrance all her own. I recalled what poets have said about a fragrant breath, hoping that it were true, but not convinced. I took it for something super-physical until I met Dulcie: breath or body, there it was: fragrance! Dulcie diffused fragrance. She is the only one I ever met who did.

They tell me that Ida of Louvain, St. Colette and St. Humiliana were as fragrant as sweet flowers. St. Herman Joseph could be traced through the corridors by the sweet perfume he scattered. St. Thomas Aquinas smelt of male frankincense. And I myself knew a lay brother who smelt of snuff. None of these explains Dulcie, who is not exclusively a saint.

There goes one serene mind in this passionate maelstrom, I thought. Such a one I was seeking when I longed for serenity, for someone who could, calm and judicious, stand outside the lists. 'How is poor old Ireland and how does she stand?' That is what I would like to find out. Not 'how is poor old Ireland and *who* is going to stand?' as MacGlornan offered; and as O'Sullivan has it that O'Leary Curtis used to inquire.

CHAPTER FOUR

'Lilli-bullero'

YES; LIKE ANOTHER Napper Tandy, but not so devoted to the bottle which produces the effect of political questionings, I wished to know, 'How is poor old Ireland and how does she stand?' I hoped to meet someone detached and serene who would give me a dispassionate account of affairs of State. Instead of that, what do you think happened? This is what I got.

There is a little passage between shops before you come quite up to Hely's. It leads to the Stag's Head. I was about to turn into it when who should be coming out but my old friend, the Senator. 'Old' he might be called, for he is past the Biblical limit, but in Ireland 'old' is more a matter of date than of decline. He was as upright and as sprightly as ever. He walked on the ball of his foot. His bright complexion had not a trace of the sallowness of age. As he extended a hand, one half of the dark, double-breasted coat he wore came with it, as if to add cordiality to the greeting.

His smiling, quizzical eye settled at last.

'Well, well, well! How's yourself?' he said.

'I can't complain.'

'You'll find a mighty lot to complain about before you are here much longer.'

Now, I like to tell myself that I am not afraid of Life, though I don't know exactly what it means. I felt something ominous in the air. I knew the Senator and I have a great *gradh* for him. He is a man of courage and of sound if somewhat vehement opinions. A man exemplary in his private life. All of a sudden he became as roused and as cryptic as McGlornan, whom I had just left. I may be unafraid of Life, but I prefer it not to come at me like an avalanche of bricks until I have some little preparation. The morning was smiling, but not so the Senator. I had become apathetic towards contemporary politics, whereas his indignation was growing every moment. At its peak point it became superhuman and impersonal, for he never mentioned a name.

He stood for a second on his toes, reminding me of the statue of the Liberator on his toes while the earth-breath came up through him in his recess in the National Bank. Here was another orator in another recess, only this recess was not between the National Bank and Dame Street, but between Dame Street and the Stag's Head.

'Get this,' he said, 'and don't you forget it. I am an old man now, but I will live to see the day when a British destroyer in the dead of night [I shivered, for I don't like the dead of night since they buried Sir John Moore] will put into Dun Laoghaire and slip that fellow away before the Irish People wake up and in their righteous wrath tear him in pieces for the way he has deceived them and for all the harm he has done to them.'

I could hear Demosthenes inveighing against the specious son of Macedon.

His nostrils ceased to dilate. He fixed me with his eye to see the effect on me of his prophetic phrensy. I had to remind myself that I was supposed not to be afraid of life. I tried to ease matters by pointing out that politics or diplomacy follow a certain pattern in given circumstances.

'The British always leave an amenable rebel with whom they can treat after an uprising. Take the case of Smuts. We have the same thing here, with this difference. . . .'

I could see the pressure oscillating in the countenance of my friend. New trains of thought were opening up for him as he dallied with the parallel.

I tried to change the subject, but I succeeded only in increasing the tension. I must have been thinking of the systolic strain, for I found myself quoting the Minister of Health.

'I see where the Minister of Health in a speech at Clonakilty talked of a band of men and women with a curious sense of loyalty who were headed by a military gentleman, a major named Quisling; and his followers are known by the newly-coined word in the international language of contempt as the Quislings.'

His eyes began to quiver like the column of mercury in the apparatus they use for taking blood-pressure. They bulged from the pressure of associations behind them. These made him for the moment speechless. There were for him so many Quislings that he could not arrange them rank by rank. He had to shake somebody, so he seized my shoulder and began to asseverate incoherently. I tried to continue with the quotation; but he thought that it was a part of my speech. I made a mighty effort to distract him from the subject that I had unwittingly brought up. I talked of a less opprobrious theme—something pleasant, for a change. When I thought that he could hear, I said genially:

'I see the President has received the ex-Prime Minister.'

'Aye You would think it was the stigmata he received.'

'The country has received them and no mistake,' I suggested, providing a wider field.

But a flash of his old wit dispelled the thunder.

'The Mikado receiving Houdini,' he suggested.

'The Mikado receiving Don Quixote would be more like it,' I replied.

'No, no,' he said. 'It's the other way about. The Mikado receiving a windmill.'

But I felt that other thoughts were fermenting. He would not remain long in his genial mood.

'Do you remember the morning that you brought Griffith and his party out to the mail-boat to meet Smuts? Griffith wanted to get a word with him before he reached Dublin Castle?'

'I do well. And I can tell you how Larry O'Neill made a fool of us all by announcing himself as the Lord Mayor of Dublin come to meet General Smuts. That was enough. The General avoided us by getting the Welsh sailors to hide him on the lifeboat deck until we went to the saloon. Then he escaped; and left us looking at Larry for a full hour. Afterwards, in the Mansion House, where there was a meeting, official this time, he advised us to have nothing to do with a Republic. He said that he had tried one and it did not work.'

'Yet he worked himself up on the ruins of one,' exclaimed the Senator, with rising colour.

'Now, now,' I said quietly. 'That's all past and done with. We must take things and persons as we find them.'

'Let me tell you, there's nothing past in this country, however it may be with South Africa. . . .'

'To proceed,' I said. 'We returned to the secret hide-out, in Dr. Farnan's house, number 5, Merrion Square. It was about half-past seven in the morning when we arrived. We were rebuked for failing to get in touch with Smuts, and we were supposed to take our failure very much to heart, when suddenly the telephone rang. His Majesty's representative in Dublin Castle was on the line. I felt like a fool, after all my preparations: meeting the Lord Mayor—who, by the way, had us nearly late—at one place; Barton at another; putting Griffith up for the night and keeping ether handy to prime the cylinders lest there should be a hitch in starting the Rolls; and then hiding my car for fear it might give away our very secret hiding-place. You should have seen Griffith's face when he found that it was little more than an annexe of Dublin Castle all the time.'

He listened eagerly, as if he had not heard it over and over again.

'It served Griffith right for expecting that he could get anything out of Smuts.'

'I can understand him for not wanting to meet disgruntled disloyalists when he was over here on a mission for His Majesty's Government. But, as I told you, the British always leave someone on the outside left to play their game subsequently.'

'They're prime boys, both of them; and Prime Ministers as a result.'

I can't bear the onus of hatred, so, in a harlequinade as it were, I asked, 'Don't you think that the pair who were receiving one another at the Vice-regal Lodge yesterday saw the humour of the situation?'

'Where's the humour in it?'

'Surely there's humour in a fellow appointing one of his pals to "receive" him; and then his pal receiving him without a wink? They must know what a pair of play-actors they are.'

'What sort of cods are the Irish People?' he asked indignantly. 'It is they who have to pay for this sort of cod.'

He is taking things rather seriously, I had to admit. Imagine taking such a bright spot as the Vice-regal Lodge seriously. He poured question after question upon me. Most of them were rhetorical, seemingly, for he did not wait for an answer.

It is hard to survey politics without being mixed in it or contaminated by it. What right have I to set myself up in the gallery and look down upon the matadors? It may be somewhat cowardly, too. For instance, I should have expostulated with him when he was talking about Smuts. After all, Smuts saw that the Republic in which he was born was an inferior type of civilisation and as cruel to the natives as the Empire which, with its marvellous powers of compromise, made him a Field Marshal. It would have started another argument—this time directed at myself—and shrunk the Senator's stream. Suppose I had asked, 'What is the Republic of Ireland doing but trying to subjugate the North? From time immemorial to the beginnings of our history Ulster was always opposed to the rest of Ireland. Queen Maeve led an army against the *Men of Ulster*, and the Hound of Ulster held it up at the ford of Ardee. It is true that the present-day men of Ulster sent out for their allies to England and to Dublin, for F. E. Smith, and the briefless Carson, saw their opportunity and used bigotry of Ulster as a spring-board to wealth and honours. Ulster has been exploited over and over again because of its gullibility once you join in the Big Walk of the Twalft.

'And, to look at it another way, is this question of Ulster, coming up as it does at the very time that the last Prime Minister was kicked out of office, anything more than a red herring drawn across the path of the present Government just to distract and fool it by crying for the moon—a well-known trick of the last leader?

'Why not leave Ulster where it has always been, separate from the rest of Ireland and, to be fair in a muddy atmosphere, a model in many respects to the rest of the country? If Ulster depends on England, so did its champion seventeen hundred years ago depend on the men of the Mersai tribe beside the present-day Liverpool (he may have been one of them) and on a suffragette named Scota?'

Had I asked such questions I might have put an end to one spate only to open another. I would not have mitigated the indignities that ate into his flesh. He did not pause for want of breath, for he seemed to breathe continuously, like the air-pump of an organ; but his words had telescoped themselves. While he was disentangling them, I thought with some misgiving, 'If politics be Life, I am taking Life too seriously.' And I recalled the remark of a famous American general who observed, while the beauty of the Veldt was being pointed out to him, from an aeroplane, 'True; but is it necessary?'

Is any government necessary? The American Colonies managed in the early stages of the war without any regular form of government—that is, if Tom Paine be right; and he was there.

As the tapping of a chisel on the skull of a patient is said to augment the anæsthesia, I could feel faintly the hammered arguments of the Senator before I was enveloped in a dream state. They were the most extraordinary dreams, too—dreams that were apparently totally unrelated to the question, to the many questions that I could no longer hear. What did I dream of? It is hard to remember. Dreams are fleeting, and few of them reach memory, few remain.

I was kissing a Bible when the court usher or crier said, 'That is not necessary.' I pushed it aside. 'Take it up.' I grew confused. If the Bible had an universal influence it would be unnecessary to kiss it; but its influence could not travel far from it if you had to hold it in your hand. How far, then, can a Bible influence one who is taking an oath? How far from the Bible is an oath binding? Obviously a Bible cannot throw its influence all over the globe as can an etherial wave; and this must be in a way a dispensation of Providence, for if the influence of a Bible were global there would be need of only one Bible. Think of all the printers that would be out of work, not to mention the missioners and the Gideon bibles in every hotel in Belfast. Philosophical systems take the place of frustrating dreams for me: philosophical systems that luckily remain incomplete and irrational as a dream itself. There must be something of the Middle Ages still in my make-up, for most of the problems by which I am confronted in dreams begin with a question—'Utrum?' as did the old theses. Whether there is more virtue in a salute from a man with a silk hat and a big head than from a man in equal social circumstances with a soft hat and a small head? Even in dream I was wary of the answer, for I could see the pitfall ahead of me, yet I could not avoid it, as is the way in dreams. Once I conceded that head and hat, I would be attributing merit to the intrinsic substance of the instrument; I would be admitting that your chances of recovery—in the case of illness—were better if your pulse were to be taken by a doctor with a gold watch than by one who had only a watch of gun-metal like that of Mr. Bernard Shaw.

And then another 'Utrum?' in the case of greeting, in the case of shaking hands—a handshake that cost the country so much a shake was obviously, if not 'better' ethically, better at any rate than that of a one-armed man, shall we say? Just as the handshakes of the late Lord Mayor, Alfie Byrne, impressed New York more than the shakes of the skipper who had navigated him over the main sea deep. They say that even the hands of the clocks were shaken in New York; and, as for the prominent members of the more or less arcane—and more prominent on that account—clubs, their hands were in slings long after he had left. Therefore you are not going to tell me that there is not some innate virtue in a hat, or a hand, or a head? Thus the tempter; but I awoke to the sound of music. Incredible as it sounds, the Senator was singing a song. It was nothing less than the old ballad that had emptied two thrones in its time when sung to a well-beaten sheepskin:

'There was an auld prophecy found in a bog,
  Lilli-bullero bullen-an ah!
That we should be ruled by an ass and a dog,
  Lilli-bullero bullen-an ah!

'The prophecy's true, and has now come to pass,
Lilli-bullero bullen-an ah!
For Talbot's the dog, and James is the ass,
Lilli-bullero bullen-an ah!
Lero, lero, lilli bulero,
Lilli-bullero bullen-an ah!'

When I looked up there was nobody there. But the refrain hung in the weather long after the singer had gone.

Do I still dream?

CHAPTER FIVE

Bridges on the Liffey !

A GREAT TRANQUILLITY IS born of a slow-flowing stream. Gradually the distemper of politics left me. After a while I cared not who manned Rathangan Fort. Even the humourless pomp and pretensions of the fantastic fellows who aped English Royalty ceased to irritate or amuse.

The greater the foolery, the greater the pomp. I thought of the Irish People to whom the Senator attributed 'righteous wrath'. I wish I could attribute to them a sense of the ridiculous, which is a precious and a salutary gift.

'Will none of you blighters ever laugh?'

Farther to the West than the spire of the Augustinians, the great brewery veiled itself in smoke. A story told by Brinsley Macnamara, that bright intellect who not only can laugh but make others laugh too, came into my mind. The story of 'The Nine Naked Arabs' he called it; and he told how nine Arabian seamen from the Persian Gulf came to the docks of Dublin on a tanker, and, hearing the word

Guinness so often repeated, took Guinness for the king of the country, and resolved, of their great courtesy, to pay their respects to such an august personage. The more they passed westward on their journey along the docks, the more the royal name was mentioned. The King's popularity was evident in that his name could be named by high and humble, lewd and learned, rich and poor. From a well-lit corner house an elderly woman emerged and, after gathering herself as for a dance, pirouetted round and round, testifying to the goodness of His Majesty. There were female dervishes, then, in this liberal country. They saw much symbolism in the greater illumination of corner houses than of others that stood in rows. His Majesty's influence extended to every corner of the earth. His name was named in every corner house.

From the bridge they could see the minarets of the great palace. When they pointed to it they were answered by many reassurances of the name. And their response was accompanied by smiles and noddings of the head.

A tall, gaunt stranger with shovel hat and hair on the upper lip tapped the ground before him as he moved towards them slowly. 'Guinness?' he asked. When they made obeisance in affirmation, he pointed with his stick to the south bank of the river. They thanked him and crossed the bridge.

They passed four bridges. The first was metalwork which spanned the river in one low arch. At length they reached a long wall of brown, baked clay topped with stone. But here there was nothing to guide them. The wall was blank. They were about to retrace their steps to the last corner house when an urchin shouted 'Is it Guinness's yez are lookin' for?' He directed them southward by the side of the wall. Gradually the ground began to rise in gentle eminence.

'Guinness?' they inquired again.

By this time many citizens escorted them, and left them at the hall door of a private house. The house of a muezzin, in all likelihood. But the house was dark and the door was shut. It was after sundown. There was nothing to do but to prostrate themselves in evening prayer and await the dawn. In a row they lay with foreheads touching the ground until the last of the curious and sympathetic citizens had gone to rest. They prayed on. After midnight, and towards that darkness that is said to come before dawn, a gentle wind arose from the south. It stirred their burnouses' many folds. An officer of the law and guardian of the great walled palace of the King patrolled the raised path, which was somewhat above the level of the street for the convenience of sentries. He regarded them with some astonishment. Then, realising that to a bi-lingual member of the city's watch nothing should be unintelligible or inexplicable, he addressed them first in the official language of the country, and met with no response. Yet he respected them as men in an attitude of prayer. After a quarter of an hour, in which the wind was rising, he grew somewhat impatient. Worship he understood. He had never for a dozen years missed a 'short twelve'; but silence he could not understand. However, thinking that they might be members of the stupid race of Sassanach, he condescended, as indeed he was often constrained to do in discharge of his duty, to speak to them with greater fluency in a Middle-Eastern dialect of English which was none other than that used throughout an Empire that includes every race under the sun except the witless who cannot comprehend the benefits of its sway.

'What d'ye think yez are doin'?' he said.

Still there was no answer. Their silence, then, was the silence of malice. 'Mute of malice.' And with that he was prepared to deal. As his truncheon descended, the wind, like a train-bearer, lifted the burnous of each kneeling figure. (Here I cover the mind's eye with a mental hand.) It was the south wind that justified the title of Brinsley's tale.

Yes; Brinsley is the last left of the men of genius whom I used to know in the old town. There was Joyce, who loved the Liffey and wrote about its rolling as no other man could. *Anna Livia Plurabelle* impressed Pat Colum because (I think he said) 133 rivers mingle with its wave. He said this in America, where Joyce is greatly esteemed for the scope of this sort of thing which his books afford: America, the home of the smoke-signal.

I know only two rivers that run into the Liffey in its course between Guinness's and the Custom House. One, I forget the name of it—Bradoge, I think—comes down from under Grangegorman Lunatic Asylum and enters Anna Liffey at the end of East Arran Street. They say that the trout in it think a lot of themselves. This megalomania may be due to their river passing under Grangegorman. The other, and this is the one that matters just now, has 'The Dolphin' disporting by its wave. You cannot see the Poddle because they have put it in a pipe. But it flows under 'The Dolphin'—you can hear it in the cellars—but it never gets into the wrong pipe.

The Corporation of Dublin did a great job in the days of George I when it built the granite walls that confine the Liffey's stream. There must have been a lot of mud and slob land before it was decided to fill in the marshes and to keep the river within bounds. And, centuries back, while it was unconfined, young men from the Dun on the south bank must have used its dark pool for a bathing-place. I remember how laboriously I tried to dig out from the Irish of *The Youthful Exploits of Finn* the story of how that son of Cumhall drowned the youths of Dublin while they were bathing in the Plain of Life! That was the way 'Liffey' was spelt then. It was wider and shallower then than the fifty yards width of it that flows unheeded now. It is discouraging to look at its course to the east, for that brings the Loop Line Bridge, with its grey steel cantilevers, into view. It is a perfect pediment for the warning 'Abandon hope'. This hideous structure shows, as plainly as if their souls could be seen, the total depravity of its promoters. It proves them to be 'utterly indisposed, disabled and made opposed to all that is spiritually good'. It reveals their abysmal ignorance, for they sinned against the Holy Ghost when they denied Beauty, which is one of the chief witnesses to the existence of God. But final impenitence was theirs, too. At the time it was proposed to build the grille across the mouth of the river which becomes nobler as it flows east, there were many citizens alive who could feel the enormity of the proposal and who spent time and money in an endeavour to prevent this outrage on the amenities of their town. But the promoters were stubborn and had their way. They knew what vulgarians were, and they knew how deep and subtile was the damage that could be done for generations to the citizens if they were to be deprived of the beauty of their expanding river, the romance of its masts and hulls lying still in the flat light.

They say that if an infant, in a foundling hospital, for instance, be left for months with a cover daily over its cot, it can never be brought up to the mental standards of the child that has been permitted to gaze about it, even though there be little comprehension in its gaze. The harm that William Martin Murphy and his gang of money-changers did to the Dubliners in depriving them forever of the view to the east can never be assessed because it has been done, and with it the power of appreciation and wonder has become atrophied. The atheists of beauty have declared themselves. This would be an old story and out of date, did it not point a moral, and point it strongly now. What happened to the Liffey then is happening to the principal street of the city now; and there are none to know the enormity of the crime, or even to recognise it for a crime at all, because have not other cities had their movie-theatres and their palaces of cement to brighten the night life of their citizens? New York has the abuse of light in the phosphorescent putrescence of Broadway and the greatest problem of juvenile delinquency of any city in the world. This may not be an example of cause and effect, but it is an example of coincidence which should not escape the notice of those who have the welfare of great cities in their keeping. Vulgarity is a form of crime because it overwhelms beauty, the harbinger of a Heaven which is always open. The fallacy of the cement palace is a message from the Father of Lies. Nothing that is born of ugliness can avail the spirit of man; nothing that can make him magnanimous or noble can come from an ugly town, any more than the infant can recover from the blotting out of its senses or the slum child forget the slum.

Those in authority would seem to have joined this conspiracy against the light. We see them dressed in black hats and in dark broadcloth, as if they would put out the light of day. Their pomp is as fallacious as the marble in the movie-halls of O'Connell Street and, worse than all, they know not what they do. They have blighted life for the people. Will these blighters never laugh? Never as long as we take them as seriously as they take themselves.

And yet there is the making of a great laugh in these playboys, a laugh that would puncture pomposity and expose humbug; for where will you see a greater farce than is enacted in these plays? Take an example:

Not long ago a miracle play was staged, not in the Rotunda, but in the Vice-regal Lodge. It was called 'The Reception'. It was a miracle play like 'Everyman'; but it had in addition another aspect of a miracle, the chief character, 'Bad Conscience' (black soft hat and black double-breasted coat), was received by one of his own creatures in a black, tall hat. It was as if a medium were to shake hands with his own ectoplasm. This seance was staged in broad daylight, for, as most of the audience were 'paper', too close a scrutiny was not expected, nor indeed was any criticism at all anticipated. There was none. There was not even a comment. Nobody asked into what Bad Conscience was received. Nobody asked how came it that, by shaking hands with himself, so to speak, an honour was bestowed on Bad Conscience. Above all, nobody asked of what was the president President. The impression presumed to exist already in the minds of the audience, and which was the condition of their being invited free to witness the performance, and which the play was designed to perpetuate, was that the two chief characters of a sovereign (*sic*) republic were affirming their sovereignty. Nobody was inclined to point out the contradiction in the terms 'sovereign' and 'republic'. Thc marionettes were Lord Rugby's Players of the Vice-regal Lodge, who are producing more contemporary plays than Lord Longford's players at the Rotunda.

These farces are staged not always by Lord Rugby. At any rate, the actors are selected once by the Irish People, and then they can arrange to keep up the caste. But they are staged with the design to fool their audience into dreaming of a false freedom which few have the courage to question or to define. Don't take this from me, for I am so prejudiced against anything that is built on humbug and deception that I am biased; but take it from this clipping from an evening paper of the city of Dublin. And from a high-court judge.

'NO TURNING BACK

'What is freedom, that freedom that is supposed to be ours in this blessed Republic? If one were to ask a keen student of the higher politics he would probably say that it was the exercise of the God-given right of man to work out his own destiny in his own country without interference from outside sources . . . Parnell said something about no man having the right to set bounds to the onward march of a nation; but the question of where the onward march happens to be leading is surely just as important as the right to march at all. We in this country have been marching onward for a quarter of a century and it is very doubtful if anybody has any clear idea of where we are making for. Practice is so different from theory. We have a Constitution setting forth a lot of lofty principles; but who will say that the ordinary citizen, the man without "pull" or friends in high places, is one whit better off or enjoys any greater measure of fair play from the Government or his financial superiors and masters than he did before Mr. de Valera presented his admiring subjects with the statement of their rights? We are all free, but at the same time we are in chains. We are taxed, directly and indirectly, to an extent that would have appeared unthinkable in the days of the Cosgrave regime. In a free country, it might be thought, there would be equal opportunities for all persons of equal merit; but in fact ability, personality and integrity of character count for nothing when a "big job" is "going" and the political jobbers take a hand in the game. The individual is hampered and restricted almost at every turn by arbitrary orders and regulations. No man, said Goldsmith, is so fond of liberty himself as not to be desirous of subjecting the will of individuals in society to his own. We are moved to these reflections by a remark of Judge Sealy at Nenagh Court when he said that the people were curtailed in every direction and that our freedom was freedom in name and not in substance. Our position amounts to this—that we have freedom to elect to power people who will deprive us of our freedom. We are free to make slaves of ourselves as we continue our interminable onward march, angrily sweeping out of the way any man who dares attempt to hold us up.'

And yet it could all be cleared away if the People would give a good guffaw in the right place. 'Will none of you blighters ever laugh?'

In the middle of the river between the bridges a cormorant appeared with a flat white fish in its bill. The fish was about six inches across, and could not be swallowed at once. The cormorant was unable to cut it in two. After shaking it violently for a while, the fish escaped, only to be caught again and brought to the surface. This went on for five minutes between the bridges in the middle of the town, and it did me good to see wild life so near the city.

The cormorant remained under the surface for a considerable time. It came up; but this time there was no fish.

I began to wonder how long it will take the Prime Minister to receive the President.

CHAPTER SIX

The Destruction Still Goes On

IGNORANCE AND APATHY are unpleasant subjects which you cannot denounce without putting yourself deliberately or unconsciously into the position of an arbiter. To ignore them makes you an accessory; nor may an Irishman by removing himself from the scene escape injury when ignorance becomes criminal, as it does when it becomes iconoclastic.

Since childhood we have heard laments for the losses of our manuscripts, our goldsmiths' work, our ancient monuments. These losses we attribute to 'the Danes'. But we abstain from any inquiry that might uncover culprits nearer home. Yet 'the Danes' did not burn Cormac's chapel; nor were they the only raiders of Clonmacnoise; nor were their hearts warmed by 'the memory of the lime-white mansions' their right hands had laid in ashes.

Every country has its upsurgings of the savage who is innate in humanity. Seldom have savages tried, as they did here, to justify their ruinous acts, much less attempt to vindicate the destruction of a nation's monuments by the pretence that they were objects that had to be removed from the path of Liberty; as if the liberty that arose from such licence could contribute to the culture of society. But when the 'liberty' purchased by the destruction of what was comely and cultured in this country becomes a retrograde movement and rewards barbarity and slavery, it is time that the pretenders were exposed and pilloried.

This is no easy task when a nation has been faced about and blinded to all that makes it worthy of a place on earth, when its standards have been thrown down and trampled, and pretence set up in the seat of principle—when, in a word, national life is founded on a lie.

It may be that in the breast of the savage there smoulders fear of everything that is beyond his understanding, and that when what was unapprehendable becomes familiar, fear turns into hate and envy of everything that is beyond his capacity. Culture, the cousin of wisdom, points an accusing finger at him. Therefore he obliterates its every trace. When the contempt of civilised nations makes him realise what a barbarian he is held to be, he will endeavour by vulgar shows to make the people he has outraged forget the destruction of their heritage. Beholding these puppet plays, we cannot refrain from asking how many 'Receptions' at the Vice-regal Lodge will compensate for the destruction of the records in the Record Office, 'that even the Danes spared'; or how many town houses must yet be turned into Government offices to compensate for the destruction of irreplaceable mansions of the country's greatest century. This inherent vandalism the poet Yeats foresaw when he advised his countrymen to:

> 'Scorn the sort now growing up
> All out of shape from toe to top,
> Their unremembering hearts and heads,
> Base-born products of base beds.'

A gang of ignoramuses, headed by a man who is cultureless, cheerless, songless and alien in every way to the kindly Irish, undertook to compensate the people for their ruined heritage by a series of imitation English Punch-and-Judy shows. It is as if a spoilt lay brother dressed in black were to present himself as the equivalent of an insulted hierarchy and a despoiled cathedral.

'Romantic Ireland's dead and gone.'

A cuckoo has usurped the songbird's nest. The songsters are cast out to perish. The tradition is broken. The song that Finn loved to hear in Letter Lee must be heard in Ireland no more.

This is the explanation of the deliberate indifference to the nation's history and the attempted substitution of trumpery pomp for national tradition.

The destruction still goes on.

In the United States the value of monuments and ancient landmarks in the march of the nation is recognised. They are cherished. Homes of great men are known and preserved. Records of the nation's great are collected. Their statues stand. The *genius loci* is honoured so that its spirit may inform the people and act as their growing inspiration through the centuries. The creative stress of those rare spirits whose lives were devoted to their fellow men is felt by all Americans in a deep and earnest mood. Britain, too, knows the worth of the example of its great sons and daughters. Whole districts are named after them. We read of the 'country' of those whose lives were spent in certain well-known parts of their native land. The houses where they dwelt are marked by entablatures. What a contrast in Ireland, where, with but very few exceptions, the birthplaces of its famous sons are unknown. How many citizens of Dublin can point out the birthplace of Swift, of Burke, or Griffith—men whose names are synonyms of human liberty? If such names cannot be associated with the spot of Irish earth their birth made sacred, what hope is there for the artists, the creators whose work made Irish culture known the world over? What hope is there for a generation whose unremembering hearts and heads are unaware of such men?

The tradition is broken.

It would seem as if the very existence of the fame of the great engendered envy and malice in the drab schemers of to-day. Not only is no effort made to preserve the names of the great, but the places that housed them or were made famous by them are razed to the ground. And the destruction still goes on apace: we read:

> 'One of the last links that bound Dean Swift with Glasnevin has been broken. The Temple in the grounds of Delville has been demolished because it stood in the way of a roadway to a new hospital. This temple, designed and built more than two hundred years ago, had, until decay set in, a medallion of Stella painted on its walls. The Latin inscription on the façade, *Fastigia despicit urbis* (it looks down on the pinnacles of the city), is said to have been suggested by Swift himself, and likely, too, for the two senses of "looks down" are in character.'

And there is another reason for regret. The Temple, as everybody called it, was built over an arched vault in which the world-famous Drapier Letters were printed. That vault, where the remains of an old printing-press were found some years ago, has been cut in two by the new road. Near the Temple stood 'Stella's bower'. That has been partially torn down. A portion of the brick, arched roof has been cut away, probably for road-filling.

> 'But the citizens will probably be compensated fully for such a trifling loss by the historical appearance of the President in his silk hat to open the new road to an old woman's Home and by the significance of this for the nation.'

The path to the future. What is it? A pathological institute.

Delville! A name composed of parts of the names of Dr. Delaney and his wife, Mary Granville. Delville, the house where thc famous men of the period met—men who were not only forerunners of the Irish Literary Renaissance but helpers in the renaissance of the soul of Ireland, men who nursed it back to life and self-respect; the house where the Delaneys entertained Addison, Thomas Parnell, Stella, Dean Swift and Thomas Sheridan. An old woman's home has taken its place. It may prove to be an appropriate refuge for whatever may be left of the spirit of the nation.

And the destruction still goes on.

In his castle of Tilira near Gort in the County of Galway some years ago, that great Irishman, Edward Martyn, was entertaining his literary friends, George Bernard Shaw, Arthur Symons, his cousin, George Moore, and, among others, the young Yeats. From a house a few miles away the widow of Sir William Gregory, an eminent Civil Servant, drove over to join the throng. Thus it came about that Lady Gregory was introduced to Yeats. That was the beginning of a partnership in letters which was to last for fifty years.

Lady Gregory's house, Coole Park, was one of the many houses to be found in County Galway. It was a three-storey house built of native limestone and dashed a light grey. Like Rafort, near Athenry, it was one of the smaller mansions of the country. But its woods were its principal attraction—the Seven Woods of Coole with their beautiful Gaelic names. They are worthy of a better word than mine. Let us hear Yeats recite his wonderful blank verse that names them all:

'I walked among the Seven Woods of Coole,
Shan-walla, where a willow-bordered pond
Gathers the wild duck from the wintry dawn;
Shady Kyle-dortha; sunnier Kyle-na-no,
Where many hundred squirrels are as happy
As though they had been hidden by green boughs
Where old age cannot find them; Pare-na-lee,
Where hazel and ash and privet blind the paths;
Dim Parc-na-carraig, where the wild bees fling
Their sudden fragrances on the green air;
Dim Parc-na-tarav, where enchanted eyes
Have seen immortal, mild, proud shadows walk;
Dim Inchy wood, that hides badger and fox;
Wise Biddy Early called the wicket wood:
Seven odours, seven murmurs, seven woods.'

In these woods walked the men who have raised the country out of that spiritual oblivion that engulfs all parochial appendages of a great Empire. On a tree in the woods their names were cut. Here Bernard Shaw went for his constitutionals; and, happily, the years have testified their advantage to his health. Here Moore was at his most mischievous on the very few occasions he was invited to Coole Park. Strange to say, it was not George Moore but Arthur Symons who deprecated the abduction of the young Yeats by the widow Gregory. When she joined the party at Tilira, Arthur Symons warned, 'Be careful of her, Willie. She has a possessive eye.' The warning availed not. Yeats went to reside at Coole; but luckily the prognostications of Symons as to the fate of Yeats's lyricism, 'She will put an end to his poetry', proved to be unfounded. Some of the best poetry he was to write was written by Yeats during his years at Coole Park. The house was magnified by his imagination into an ideal Irish mansion full of the courtliness of a century it may not have seen at all. His imagination endowed it with the traditions of the period he most admired, that century in which the Anglo-Irish mind flowered and 'the salt of the earth', as he called them, enunciated opinions, liberal for their period and since unexcelled.

What has been done to preserve these memories? A saw-mill marks the site of Coole and its Seven

Woods. The very stones and slates of the house that welcomed the greatest geniuses of their generation have been removed by a contractor (building materials are scarce) to build an ecclesiastical structure within the walls of the disused Galway gaol. How truly Yeats's friend, George Russell (Æ), said: 'One of the very first symptoms of the loss of the soul of a nation is the loss of the sense of beauty.'

Someone, not unmindful of the fame of Coole, bought its hall-door for five pounds ($12). From it he cut a heart-shaped piece of wood which held the knocker. This he offered to the Dublin Municipal Gallery. It was refused because, no doubt, those who conducted a gallery of Ireland's great did not want such a stultifying reminder of the many acts of vandalism against 'the noblest of the things that are gone'.

'The President has received the ex-Prime Minister at the Vice-regal Lodge.'—Daily paper.

When I consider the drabness—drab as the sodden peat in the Park—and the soullessness of the present State, the paradox that puzzled me is resolved. The paradox was this: why did that efflorescence which is called the Irish Literary Renaissance manifest itself while the country was directly under British rule? The answer is that those engaged in the Irish Literary Movement drew their inspiration directly from an unbroken tradition, from the sagas, the legends and the speech of the country. There was no pretence about it. The undiluted language of the Gael was theirs. The old tongue had not been pidginised into a political shibboleth. Then, too, there was adventure in the air. Without adventure there is stagnation. The sagas had a vitalising effect on those who listened to them. They renewed the national spirit with a love that was genuine, strong and impassioned; poets became patriots and, in turn, poets made patriots. The soul of the nation, so long silenced and alienated by the denationalising system of education known as the Intermediate System, burst into song. The issues were clear-cut. The enemy was British domination with its universality or Imperialism, which, like a ten-cent store, was to contain everything reduced to one level (and nothing worth much) under one management or administration, an Emporium of Empire. The defence against this levelling was a return to nationalism, a recoil from Imperialism. There can be neither art nor poetry in a regime that is founded on politics which has debauched the very language of the country into ersatz Gaelic that is a confessed failure:

> 'Mr. T. Derrig, Minister for Education, told General Mulcahy that eight essays had been received for a $500 competition in Irish on the life and works of Thomas Davis. The adjudicators did not consider that any of the essays was

of sufficiently high standard to justify the award of the prizes.'

And this after twenty years of compulsory Irish! There is as much spent on this attempt to spell English in Irish characters—Bus, Incoim Tax, Telephon and Phuist—as would clear the disgraceful slums of our towns and raise the standards of living to include cleanliness, health and self-respect; or to perpetuate, by the preservation of their homes, the glory of our great men.

There are certain things that may not be justly compared with one another. For instance, it is not just to compare the cost of women's imitation jewellery with the cost of demolishing slums. They are not in the same category. But the cost of a tinsel court may be compared with the cost of slum-clearing because they are under the same dispensation, and that public; and the same men have the allocation of the money. Lately, some years ago, they were endeavouring to increase their own salaries, although not one of them, according to the then Prime Minister (and he magnanimously included himself), is worth more than £1,000 ($5,000) a year.

From the ends of the earth men come, are 'received' and find a home in an Irish 'republic', where a great number of its citizens have not a home of their own.

'Will none of you blighters ever laugh?'

CHAPTER SEVEN

Opposites

PLEASE FORGIVE ME for breaking off so abruptly in the last chapter. The fact is I could not help it. I got the hell of a shock. Suddenly out of my Stream (the Conscious or Unconscious, it is much the same to me) arose, came into mind, awful thoughts, like a litter of half-drowned pups coming up to accuse their owner. The thoughts had to do with people who go on denouncing others or hating them and what they stood for, and so forth. I began to recall things I had heard and read on the subject of self-righteous reformers just as I was becoming one myself.

This is the first quotation I remembered:

> 'The perfect men of the present day, however, are not constituted thus. They love to be sharp upon the faults of others and lenient towards their own, the result being that no advantage accrues to either. In their own conduct they are satisfied with a minimum of virtue and

ability, cajoling others as well as themselves into believing this more than it is. But when it comes to estimating anyone else's virtue and ability, nothing seems good enough for them. The past is raked up and the present ignored. . . .'

Now, that's the very thing I have been doing, being sharp upon the faults of others and easy on my own, with the implication that I could do things much better, and that I am a better man. And this, mark you, after denouncing the whole tribe of ward heelers. As for raking up the past, I even went farther back than the ex-Premier himself, who usually begins at Brian Boru. I must say that I felt a bit guilty, and was trying to acknowledge it to myself, when up came another, and this time a worse and more alarming memory. It came from George Russell (Æ), the Sage of Rathgar:

> 'There is a law in human Nature which draws us to be like that which we passionately condemn.'

And there is a bar-tender in New York who told me that in the Speakeasy days he was up so often before the beak that he began to look like him.

When these two revelations hit me together, I passed into shock. I wonder if I shall ever pass out of it—that business of being drawn to be like and, worse still, of looking like one whom I 'passionately condemn'. What would the Senator say if he met me metamorphosed walking down Dame Street? I don't know if this transposition includes having a body-guard; but I know that if it happened to me, I wouldn't care who took a pot shot at me. The sooner I got it over the better. But, holy smoke! what an escape! I wouldn't so much mind being turned into Sean T. about dinner-time, provided that I could snap out of it when the guests were going home. But!

The only thing to exorcise me and to prevent the other ghastly possibility is to go and get a large whiskey and a little water. That's a stream my opposite or ghoul will never cross. From this on I will stop passionately condemning anybody. I am quite satisfied, perhaps too much so, with being myself.

I never before realised the wisdom of 'Love your neighbours'.

As I went my way towards the Dolphin on the Poddle, I took a surreptitious look at my hat. It was still grey, not black. Thank God! And I was still compact and middle-sized. But I felt strangely depressed. I took another look at myself in a copper bed-warmer in McBirney, the haberdasher's window. I made due allowance for the colour and the distortion, yet I resembled the Knight of the Rueful

Countenance just a little bit. But when I meet Jack Nugent I will be all right. To be 'received' by him means something.

Outwardly, the Dolphin consists of brick walls, Victorian bricks and terra-cotta ornaments. There are nine weathercocks on the roof which can account for any wind. The Later Alcoholic style, appropriate enough for a tavern. Otherwise it has nothing to recommend it architecturally but a beautiful metal knocker. However, brick walls do not the Dolphin make. It is Jack Nugent and the boys within. What was it Dr. Johnson said about there being more joy found in a well-run tavern than in anything else Man's ingenuity invented? Jack Nugent can tell you more about that than the learned doctor.

Jack Nugent is a pleasant, portly, welcoming man with a kind of chortle. When he laughs, he turns sideways, with his hand over his mouth, for his laughter ends in a fit of coughing. He often coughs without a cold. He has a retreating chin; but he wears an open collar for emergencies so that his necks may come to its aid. Sean T. has an open collar, too; but I don't think that either of them has been denouncing the other. It must have something to do with greeting and goodwill. Jack's mind is full of weights and dates and considerations of form. He is a hierophant in Ireland's oldest religion, which is the Cult of the Horse. Anyone who knows anything about reverence, not to mention good manners, knows that when an owner of all people is in conferencce with an expert on form it is no time to butt in with an interruption or a shout, as it happened once. The Earl of Fitzwilliam was in deep consultation with Jack Nugent at the foot of the stairs when who should come out but Jerry Cattermole shouting:

'There's no soap in your toilet, Nugent!'

The owner of the Dolphin turned on him with righteous indignation. His necks rushed reinforcements to his chin, which stood firm and did not retreat.

'Get out of here! How dare you come into any man's house with dirty hands? Go home and wash yourself!'

After giving this advice conversation was resumed quietly with the Earl.

Anyone who does not go to the Dolphin in Dublin is hardly worth seeking. To put it another way, anyone whom Jack Nugent does not know is not worth knowing. You may be sure of one thing: he is not a sportsman. This statement should be qualified a little. There are judges who, probably in order to preserve the adage, 'Sober as a judge', do their drinking privately at their clubs, at the King's Inns or in one another's houses; but not in the

Dolphin. Then there are doctors who regard it as unseemly to be seen drinking in a public place. In the case of judges there is one exception. Judge Meredith was well known to Jack Nugent, not because he was a judge, but because he won the quarter-mile championship in his day and Jack's day, for Jack held the billiard championship for years.

To go back to Judge Meredith. I can still see his white calves twinkling as they carried his slight, flat body swiftly round the green of College Park. Even on grass he could always break two minutes for the quarter. Jack could tell you his times. The Judge was a scholar, a philosopher, a great student of Hegel. Maybe it was owing to the Hegelian dialectic that he could not make up his mind. If he began by being lenient to a prisoner at the beginning of a trial, he compensated for it by downing him at the end. So notorious was his vacillation that his architect disobeyed instructions and put only one toilet instead of two at the stairhead of his new house. The Judge had to acknowledge the wisdom of the omission and to accept the architect's explanation, 'In the case of an emergency, Judge, you might fall between two stools.'

With those whom Jack Nugent does not like there must be something very wrong. Their names are on a lot of dusty telegrams in a glass case in the hall to the left as you come in. They have been addressed to men who died in Jack's opinion, men who failed to live up to the easy standards required of sportsmen, so their telegrams are their obituary notices.

Still talking of decent fellows, I remember late one evening, when I was having supper in the Dolphin, I felt an arm about my shoulders and heard a throaty voice in my ear. It was mine host acknowledging me and welcoming me home. We talked of old times and of old friends: what Irishman does not love to muster them in his talk? When I came to Jimmy Montgomery, the Master of the Dolphin was silent. Slowly he shook his head. That was enough. I knew that my old friend Jimmy Montgomery, the Film Censor, had passed away. In a moment Jack Nugent changed from his solemnity and smiled.

'Did you hear this one?' he asked. 'The boys went to see Jimmy as he lay dying. "How are you, Jimmy?" they said. "Just hovering between wife and death," said Jimmy with a smile.'

What better epitaph could a man have than a moment's solemnity, and then a laugh? I often heard Jimmy telling us how he had reversed the usual procedure and had drunken up the two public-houses his father left him.

I remember his reply when he was asked what he wanted on a certain anniversary.

'Two minutes silence.'

Jack Nugent sighed as he parted from me:

'Jimmy Montgomery was a grand fellow!'

A fine testimonial from a man who knows form so well.

But there are other decent fellows who are dead and gone. Happy Harry, whose speech was a series of propagating adjectives with an unvaried noun to give the adjectives an hold, is no longer at his table near the door.

Tall, striking Fred Weston, with a large, aquiline, embossed nose that perversely recalled Mr. Gladstone, surveys the scene no more: dead as Jack Lister, who used to lean across a sidecar with the sun on his patent-leather shoes. All with the 'also rans'. They will have an anxious time in Heaven balancing weights against the jockeys' wings.

Amid the talkative throng you can find the habitués of the day. If you cannot, your foreground is not right. You will be more sib to them if you are going to Punchestown, Leopardstown, The Curragh or Baldoyle. There's the gallon Baron, with his race-glasses slung slantwise. He is too careful to trust them to the hat-rack, for there is no knowing if a tout or two may not have escaped the waiters' watchful eye, because on a day like this, when there is a rush of people coming and going in and out, it might be quite easy to slip a pair of race-glasses off just as you were taking down your raincoat. So the Baron explains with modern instances. 'Excuse me,' you plead, 'there's Hugh Harpur and Dudley Walsh,' which only makes it worse, for the Baron knows them all, and they know the Baron. They are not going to the races. No. They will keep on lunching instead, anchored by the conviction that they are too busy to go anywhere.

While I was looking in at the door, Willie slid as if he were on skis.

'You'll have a seat in a minute, sir. Jack's in York; but expected back to-night.'

His whisper was audible, though it came from a corner of his mouth.

I had to tell Willie that I didn't want a seat. I turned instead back to the left-hand bar off the entrance, where they serve lunch and drinks off the Aberdeen granite that is curved like a horse-shoe.

I am still a bit shaky after my narrow escape. The surest way to be different from anything I passionately condemned is to order myself a large Jameson and Thwaites for luck, since soda-water was invented in Sackville Street and Jameson is distilled in Bow Lane. Tom is sympathetic. You would think it was only yesterday I left the Dolphin.

'You may fill it up. Ha! That's the stuff. Tom, give us another just to make sure.'

I stopped.

Tom looked at me. He must be wondering what it was I wanted to make sure.

Pondering on such things, I was roused by an intense whisper from Tom: 'Dan Chaucer is good at four to one.' So Tom confided, having looked sharply from left to right. 'The third or fourth race; but you'll see it on your card.'

'Dan Chaucer me arse,' an unconsulted little citizen beside me remarks contemptuously.

His speech was in idiom, so I need not set his words down literally. I would have ignored the remark had I not known that, long before Freud, the Irish attributed negative properties to the lower portion of the alimentary tract. I took his comment as a negation of the barman's faith. It meant that, in the citizen's opinion, it was not only improbable but impossible that Dan Chaucer would win the third or fourth race. A copper-faced client on my right, who looked like something from the Levant, announced that not only did he own but that he trained Dusty Miller.

'Don't mind them,' the bar-tender said. 'Don't mind either of them. They only come in here to try to pick up a few tips. Did ye see how quick the little fellow was to pick up what I whispered to you?'

What would the poet Chaucer have thought had it been revealed to him that part of his fame would be to have a race-horse named after him in Irlonde?

And what would he have thought of the manners and customs of the modern Irish had he heard his name qualifying a word which, though he did not hesitate to employ it in his verse, lacked both dignity and respect even in his day?

As I sipped my antidote the problem of the names of race-horses bubbled up. How is it that their names in the aggregate come to denote race-horses and not running dogs, the names of which are as odd and fanciful, yet in some subtile way associated only with canine, and not equine owners. This problem kept me brooding until another question arose, and one that was not easily solved. It was this. How do they who name horses prevent them from being associated—by mistake, of course—with the products of Shanks in Barrhead, Scotland or Murray Crane in the U.S.A., manufacturers of toilet utensils both? How, in a word, is one to know that Adamant by Hanley out of Twyford, Ailsa, or Deluge, or Ladore or, more ambitiously, Niagara, are not to be looked for in hotel toilets rather than in paddocks? I confess that the problem baffled me. If it baffles me, it will baffle these touts, I thought. If I could have a word with Tom that would not be listened to by Copper Face or the commentator on Chaucer, something might be done. While one of the barmaids was cutting ham and trying to obey directions from Chaucer, I got Tom to the end of the bar.

'You know Shanks' patent urinals in the lavatory?' I asked.

Tom looked blank; a puzzled smile: then he nodded.

'How about giving me a tip to back "Shanks' Pat"? It's only a urinal; but it sounds like a winner!'

I left it to Tom and went back to my stool.

I was tracing the change of the times in the changes in the names of horses. In the days of unsung Victoria only classical or famous names, like the names of battles, were used in designating horses. You would almost trace their date from their names. Omdurman, Sevastopol, Khartoum. Then came the double names, and with them the decline; names such as Pay Parade, Goodwin Sands, Fleet Street, White Lodge . . . Tom whispered audibly:

'Here's something for your ear only. You can get a hundred to one now on Shanks' Pat for next year's Derby. Orby was not much of a sire, but Shanks' Pat has his dam's and Tetrarch's blood, and not a bloody word about it. He's not even listed yet.'

'Where can he be seen?' I asked.

Tom said mysteriously, 'That would be telling ye!'

Though the little fellow used no note-book, I could see that the tip had registered.

It registered on my other side, too, for Addis Ababa gave himself away by asking, 'Wot's this about Orby being a bad sire?'

'This is doing me good,' I said: and I went on thinking of the romance that is mixed up in the names of race-horses. I know how Bahram got his name from that great hunter. The Aga Khan could not have given his winner a better name. It fetched even me, who rarely mix gold with the Olympic dust. But I bet on Bahram, for I knew that he was as swift as the wild ass and that he could not lose. And wasn't I right?

Then there are fanciful names by which the fancy women of the less austere owners endowed their lovers' steeds, names which reveal the trend, and sometimes the limitations, of the ladies' imagination. Sometimes the owner names his horse after his lady, Lovely Anne. Sometimes the lady returns the compliment, as in the case of the French horse, Monsieur L'Amiral. Charming! I wonder what the old sea-dog said when she insisted on her whim. Sometimes ladies call horses after the pet name of their lovers. This is the only explanation of how No Nightie got its name.

Brands of champagne are used and names of cigars; both associated with racing women and men. Château Yquem, which those for it who go to the races will pronounce in their own way; just as

Elysium can come to betray to the bookies who have their personal pronunciation the name of its owner's sweetheart, Alice. So, too, Euphegenia tells to all in the know that Fred Weston went round with Jenny Hughes. . . .

'Excuse me, Mister,' the fellow on my left said deferentially. 'Don't think that I want to butt in. There'll be no getting it out of Tom, and the Derby's off almost a year. So there'll be very little harm in letting a fellow know who owns Shanks' Pat.'

I assumed the look of one whose confidence is more or less outraged. Then I softened somewhat and, with adjurations to the profoundest secrecy, not to mention mystery, I revealed the fact that Shanks' Pat was owned by a very high official of the Dail who, for conscientious reasons, could not enter it in his own name. The last part of my confidence convinced him. He had swallowed Tom's tip, toilet and all. Lest I might think that I had conveyed anything of an important nature, he said indignantly:

'Why the hell can't he run it in his own name? Doesn't he and his bunch get seven and a half per cent out of every bet? And why the hell can't he go to a race meeting, like every honest bloke in the country?'

'There I leave you!' was all I said.

Brave men are these gamblers. They blame themselves for their errors of judgement. They never blame the horse. They lose or win the making of a life of luxury and ease, yet they never pause to seize the prize. It all goes back into 'the field'. True votaries, their devotion never relaxes. Their courage never faints. For them is no fascination equal to the fascination of life and death when all is put to the touch. Their deity gives and takes away. Blessed be the name of the Horse!

Thinking thus, I was reminded of a tale told by Jake Brennan, of a gambler who for the nonce had lost his all. He was rolling down Park Avenue in New York some hours before the dawn. He was homeless. His eye caught a notice on one of the fashionable churches, 'Enter by the north court'. He entered, and fell asleep in one of the pews. When he awoke a funeral service was in full swing: flowers and candles. Turning to a lady of quality on his left, he asked, using Happy Harry's only adjective, which implies a certain disapprobation of the less fortuitous aspects of Life, 'Did you ever see so many . . . candles?' Her look knocked him unconscious again. On recovering, he inquired this time concerning the multitude of flowers. Again he passed out, to be wakened by a stentorian voice intoning loudly:

'The Lord gave and the Lord hath taken away.'

He brightened and, turning again to the lady, said:

'Well, if that isn't a fair shake, I'll . . .'

And he reverted to that Chaucerian usage of which we have already adumbrated.

So to the gambler the giving and the taking away are both parts of the game. It's a fair shake. That is all they ask, though the dice may favour them but once in twenty shakes.

Is it any wonder that the Dolphin should observe secrecy of a cult so important? Or that the principal shrine in Ireland of the horse should have its mysteries: mysteries concerning form, weights, tips, ownership, and mystery surrounding the movements of its priest whom Willie whispered was 'expected back' from York?

If the Dolphin be the shrine of mystery, do not forget that it is also the temple of Hope. Jack may be back from York 'any minute now'.

CHAPTER EIGHT

Lewd and Learned

A WOMAN WAS SCOURGED in the House of Industry for some infringement of the rules. The Board met, and found that the porter whose duty it was to inflict such punishment as the Board awarded had been remiss in his duty. He was ordered to scourge the woman again, more 'conscientiously' this time, which meant more heartlessly; and he was fined a week's pay. His pay was six shillings and sixpence a week. A clergyman was a member of the Board. The porter was not as conscientious as the clergyman. This was in Dublin in the XVIIIth century, a century of magnificence and squalor, of 'Mud and Purple', as the poet O'Sullivan has it, a century of the most dehumanising existence for the paupers of Dublin and of every other town in the kingdom.

This was one of the most inhuman centuries of which there is indubitable record. It was the century of floggings unto death in the King's Navy. It was the century in which women were stripped and scourged in the lazar-houses and the pestilential prisons. The century in which the insane were chained and bedded on straw and exhibited to make an holiday. A century in which the death penalty was inflicted for an hundred offences. Much of this inhumanity is a thing of the past. The gaols of Ireland and England are the only places that still retain a remnant of the tradition. And the slums of the city still bear witness to the festering lives of the XVIIIth-century poor. Yet during that period Dublin arose in stately buildings and gracious private houses unapproached for the beauty and the symmetry of their design. So out of the misery and suffering came the Pyramids of Egypt and the victories of the Nile and Trafalgar. Architecture outran hygiene in Dublin as well as at Versailles.

To one of the best examples of XVIIIth-century architecture in Dublin, the Provost's House, I was bidden to meet the Provost and, with the American Minister, go with him to dine at what used to be the Chief Secretary's Lodge in the Phoenix Park.

The Provost is Dr. Alton, a robust, restless man of middle height, which makes him all the more burly, oak-complexioned, robust, but not stalwart, a stout fellow who looks before and after. He looks *after* in his study of Ovid, on whom he is an authority; and *before* in that he has foreseen the future of Anglo-

American culture. For this he plans to make provision by extending the present great library of Dublin University to accommodate American as well as British literature. But, like most of those who plan for the future, he lacks present funds. And yet years hence there will be a great discovery. Someone else will adopt—and plagiarise—the Provost's ideas, and not only be hailed as a foreseeing statesman, but be given ample funds to cement America and Great Britain and bridge the Atlantic by an intellectual bridge. This would bridge the estranging sea more lastingly and advantageously than any bridge of boats or aeroplanes. For Ireland it would be a peculiar advantage because to the fluency and grace of the English language as it is spoken in Dublin, it would add the vigour and imagination of the language as it is used in the United States. That language will expand in power and poetry with the growing power and expansion of the United States. Is it too much to prophesy, looking back at the old landmarks, that this will lead to unimaginable evolutions of art and literature?

This is what the far-seeing Provost has in mind. May success crown his plans for an Anglo-American library on Irish soil where one of the world's greatest libraries already stands. Thus he looks before.

In his looking after I am interested, too. Concerning his predilection for that sprightly fellow, Ovid, psychiatrists, who see far more than I would care to, might tell us that if the Provost had his way, and could control time and space and public opinion, he would choose to be Ovid. For this, of course, he would require to be born in imperial Rome about the time that the Emperor Augustus was becoming grandfatherly, respectable, and so censorious, and beginning to dodder. That was about the time that Ovid was rumoured to have spied on that other Julia, the Emperor's grand-daughter, as she was reclining in her bath. Yes, he would have to go back, for I cannot imagine anyone spying on a relative of anyone in power in Dublin who may be said, when allowances are made and mean things compared with great, to be in a position tantamount to that of Augustus—doddering apart. No, Siree! This ejaculation must have arisen from my subconscious. The Emperor, as is well known, banished the poet to barbarous and half-illiterate Tomi. Our censorious gaffer has gone one better: he has banished Tomi into Dublin.

But to return to Alton and Ovid. We left him spying on Julia, an action that is in direct contradiction to the advice the poet gives us in his *Ars amatoria*, 'Never spy on a woman'. I cannot see the Provost doing any such thing. He must have been inspecting the bath to assure himself that it was properly steam-heated, for I noticed his concern lest he catch cold.

He has this in common with the poet: an interest in temperature.

He showed me parts of the Provost's House in which I had never been. He pointed out portraits which I had never seen. It was years since I was entertained by any Provost: admonishment cannot be called entertainment.

He demonstrated the white paint which had been applied to a Chippendale bookcase during a preceding consulate. The moral adduced was that paint could be taken as an index to taste. I remarked, 'It was *not* Mahaffy!'; and for once I was uncorrected in the Provost's house.

From the drawing-room, with its cylindical ceiling and its columns topped with cornutes of gold, we descended to rooms below from which terraced lawns could be seen smooth-shaven and rolled, as they had been for decade upon decade. It was getting late. Soon the car would come to take us to dinner in the Phoenix Park.

From the finest example of an XVIIIth-century mansion left in the city, we drove along the slums which marked the nadir of that time. We were still in that century, in spite of electric cars, taxis and telephones. It is the mentality of a town that marks its date. I have been in prehistoric settlements which nobody has discovered in spite of their electric light. I am in the XVIIIth century still.

The Minister lives in the lesser of the two magnificent houses which were built when the English satraps ruled the land. They were built with true British soundness, and were comfortable and well proportioned, built with all the liberality which is associated with England, and which is undiminished by subject nations having to foot the bill.

The Chief Secretary's Lodge lies less than half a mile west of the Vice-regal Lodge. Though neither as large nor as well endowed with garden, lawns and ornamental water, the Chief Secretary's Lodge is commodious and comfortable. It is separated to the south by a sunk fence from a large field which is called the Fifteen Acres, though actually it is nearer 150 acres in extent. It enjoys the same view across the Liffey Valley of the Dublin mountains as the larger mansion. The Chief Secretary was any official whom the British Government of the time saw fit to rule Ireland. His appointment was political.

The Provost and I met some very pleasant people at dinner in the Lodge. How pleasant and charming or who they were, I do not think it advisable to write, because, just at this moment, while the cult is in favour of 'the Common People', pleasant and cultivated people are called 'the Ascendancy'. I have never met anyone who confessed that he was a common person, though I cannot avoid meeting many who are champions of the Common People. So it is hard to say whether or not I would like common people whom I have never met. I have met one or two who prefaced their remarks by 'speaking as a plain man'; and I will admit that the role was appropriate. I don't know why they choose plainness or what prevents them from admiring the Ascendancy, who comprise the best people I have met. I know that they are called 'the Best People', but it is said derisively. Derision does not affect me (I sometimes deal in it myself). Being called a snob does not affect me; so I am quite eligible to admire the Best People.

We had a very pleasant evening. The best of Dublin in the person of the Provost; and the best of Ireland in the person of the Minister's guests; and the best of the United States in the person of his wife and the wife of one of his guests. In the middle of the entertainment I reflected sadly how few of our citizens had the moral courage to like 'the Best People'. These are rarely dull. They never look cadaverous and offer it up to Ireland. They are always cheerful, even in adversity, because their courage is high. Like the best people in England, they cannot understand defeat. That is why I suspect they look upon the present regime as just a bore; pitiable and passing. I don't want to give them away to the head-hunters, for from them has come anything that, for the last two centuries, has redounded to Ireland's culture amid the civilisation of Europe. The head-hunters have still the same idea as the Common People had in the days when Quarles wrote:

> ' We'll drive the doctors out of doors,
> And arts, whate'er they be,
> We'll cry both arts and learning down,
> So, hey, then up go we!'

I don't want anyone to join this kind of ascendancy at the Best People's expense.

I left the house of the liberal and genial man who represented a great Republic.

The relation of a country's politics to the potential power of its best citizens is a theme which historians have not presented as a natural phenomenon. Yet for the greater part of the life of a constitutionally governed country and the whole life of a country suffering under a dictator the best brains have not been available to conduct the fortunes of their country. This would seem to be in the nature of things generally. It is in the nature of politics particularly. ' The inevitable tendency of the higher intelligence in all countries has been to separate itself from the practical concerns of men,' so W. K. Magee says.

Maybe this is all for the better, if not for the best. Think of what happened to Plato, one of the world's greatest intellects—sold in Ægina as a slave because he bored Dionysius the tyrant with his plan for an impossible Republic; and to come to our own day, think, if you can, what would happen to a city run by Bernard Shaw: it would be all a Convent Garden. It is not fair to expect that the best brains should represent a nation. This would leave all but kindred intelligences unrepresented. No; there must be a mediocre mind to represent what is the bulk of any nation: mediocrity. The higher the mediocrity, the better. Avoid the best, therefore, as you would eschew the worst.

Yet there were times when devotion to the common weal was the noblest aim and occupation of a nobleman's life. With the Cult of the Common People an awful fate looms over the Common People. It is that they may attempt to govern themselves. What have they to offer themselves but commonness? This they avow. The results of it in practice are as bad as the worst outrages against human liberty tyrants have perpetrated, because they may be disciplined only by 'liquidation'. But this is a lesson that may not be learned, because when the Common People become Communists they are herded and driven by their worst elements until they find themselves under a dictatorship as avaricious and as cruel as the ideals that distracted them were deceptive and destructive. It would seem as if politics have become the perquisite of certain banded vagrants who hate every evidence of civilisation and the humanities which proceed from civilisation. To politicians such as these, educated and self-disciplined persons do not appeal. These are 'the Enemies of the People'. And, in turn, the best and most liberal minds in the nation loathe and are repelled by the exhibition of narrowness and chicanery of those in power. Thus a nation is doomed to be divided and doomed to be led by its least competent and most unworthy citizens. Proof of this lies round us. Can the problem be solved? Very recent history gives a solution of the disparity between the competence of politicians and the specialised activities of devoted men. The common danger of the last war drew every American citizen into an united defence organisation in which the brains of the whole nation were pooled, regardless of personal avocations or opinions. For this, a threat to the existence of the nation is required. There was no such menace to Ireland, because England held over her subjects a protecting shield. Ireland, despite the mouthings of its politicians, has to be protected by British arms for military and economic considerations.

Another thought, probably a reaction to the pleasant evening, came to make me sad. Why is Ireland so susceptible to catchwords and demagogues? Why does she suffer aliens sometimes to take over her Government and to dictate to her, and make her resent the existence of the best citizens in the land? Yet there was a time—a time within my recollection—when the services of the most representative men of Ireland were availed of when the Senate was founded by William Cosgrave. True, it was under an agreement with Great Britain that one-quarter of the Senate was to consist of such men. This to President Cosgrave was no duress. That statesman saw clearly that no country could give an account of itself with its right hand tied behind its back. So he appointed such men as Jameson, Guinness, Lords Glenavy, Mayo, Granard, Headfort, etc., and the poet Yeats, who represented the spirit of the nation as no other man of his time could or did.

The reactionaries and the Little Irelander from foreign parts came into power, and the Senate was abolished. Then, when the Prime Minister at the time had contradicted himself sufficiently, it was established again. The nation waits until its rulers are over-ripe or rotten enough to drop off the bough. Ireland outruns its Government every ten years.

Instead of twenty-five per cent of men who had a stake in their country, there were fifty per cent of persons with outlandish names in the last Government, none of whom had any stake in the country; all of whom owe their position to fomenting hate and class hatred, farmers of grievances; all wavers of a red flag to the Brown Bull.

To find an answer to this and similar problems I had, first, to define what is meant by 'Ireland'; and then to suspend myself fairly (if I could) between the Best People and the Common Man. The result of this investigation was not comfortable. I saw the same force at work as that which turned Russia into a movable camp of slaves: the same undiscriminating pursuit of impractical ideas: the menace there and danger thereof; the imminence of that danger and its inevitability.

Absit omen.

CHAPTER NINE

A House in a Garden

TO RESTORE MY benignity I will go to Connemara. But I remembered Best's invitation. This will do just as well. I can postpone my departure to the Many-Coloured Land. I will go to visit Best this evening.

Best lives in 57, Upper Leeson Street, in one of those houses set far back from the highway with a garden in front and a garden at the rear. It belongs to a period when men insisted on space and privacy and life was unconfined.

He saw me as I walked up the garden path, and he opened the door before I had ascended the seven steps to the hall. The rooms on the right had the folding doors between them removed so that the rooms formed one long chamber with a view of flowering-trees and shrubs fore and aft. Laburnum and lilac leant over the path in the front garden. You could see fruit-trees flowering in the garden at the back. And the house was silent, as becomes a scholar's dwelling.

On a mantelpiece of black marble stood a Renaissance copy of the IVth century B.C. statuette of the Listening Dionysius, from the collection of the late Sir Thornley Stoker, who never tolerated anything but ' a genuine piece '.

Best's memory was better than mine; but we failed to recall an intimate name. Mrs. Best in her quiet voice recalled it for us; and so the memory of old acquaintances flowed on.

' First, let me thank you for the notes you sent me of George Moore's funeral, and particularly of the funeral oration composed by Æ and delivered by you while workmen were laying Moore's ashes in the cyst. You got my version of the proceedings from Lennox Robinson? I gave him my article for you when I met him in the Waldorf Astoria in New York.'

Best hesitated a moment.

' I never got it,' he said.

I was taken aback. I had counted so much on Best getting the first copy of *Town and Country*, in which the article appeared. I was irritated. I assured Best that the last thing I did in the Waldorf was to put the magazine in Lennox's suitcase. This was early in the morning, before he set out for Europe. I apologised, and promised to write to London to ask him what he had done with it.

We talked of the eccentric funeral, and of Colonel

Moore's difficulty in conducting a pagan ceremony in the middle of Catholic Mayo; and of the post-mortem pleasure George Moore must have felt (if ashes could be sentient) in putting his friends, and especially his religious brother, into such a predicament.

Lennox irritated me in another way. When I asked him when Yeats's remains were to be brought back from Cap Martin to Sligo, as he had willed, Lennox waived the question with, 'I don't see why anything should be "brought back".' Yet the French Government offered a battle-ship to carry the remains. That was an honour; and an acknowledgment of what the French thought of Yeats. More than his own countrymen, it seemed. Are we to make an exhibition of our boorishness and betray our inability to appreciate great art by not accepting this fine and generous offer of the French Government?

'Which French Government?' Lennox asked; and he went on handing out the sandwiches.

Best pondered. He had been unaware that the French had offered a battle-ship. He did not reply. He did not comment. Possibly he was wondering who would undertake the removal of the remains. I am sure that he expected nothing of the last Government. He would be right in that, for Yeats had denounced those in office and all their works shortly before he died: 'And great Art beaten down'. Anyway, I said:

'It is very hard to be angry with Lennox. He told me an amusing and characteristic story of Yeats when their friends had arranged a reconciliation between Yeats and the poet Seumas O'Sullivan. For some reason or other they had never cottoned to one another, as you know. You know, too, how Æ, in the kindness of his heart, had tried to persuade Yeats to encourage the younger poet, and the answer: "Where is the wild dog which ever praised his fleas?"

'O'Sullivan's repartee has not had such a wide publicity.'

'What was it?'

'"Where is the wild dog which ever knew its father?"

'Probably it was tartness such as this that kept the men apart. Be that as it may, years later the day came when all was arranged. Yeats and O'Sullivan were to meet at some party in the Abbey Theatre and to be reconciled. Horace Reynolds, the author from Boston who knows more about Yeats and his writings than any Irishman, was a guest. Lennox told how that day Yeats had gone to the dentist to have a tooth extracted. But I cannot pretend to tell the story as Lennox tells it with his persuasive and unemphatic voice.'

'Do your best.'

'Lennox described how Yeats, who was to some extent an hæmophiliac, frightened the dentist by bleeding continuously after the extraction; and how the dentist put him in a bedroom upstairs, and then went out to dine and forgot about him. After dinner he suddenly remembered Yeats, who had a strange faculty for resigning himself to such circumstances, abandoned in the bedroom. He rushed back and released his patient. That explained why Yeats was very late in coming to the meeting. At last he arrived. He blinked in the light. Then he remembered the purpose of the party and, going over to *Horace Reynolds*, shook his hand and from the highest rung of his personality said, "O'Sullivan, I am glad to meet you after all these years."

'I asked Lennox if it was put on as a pose.'

'Was it?' Best asked.

'Lennox does not think so. He attributed it to the dope or whatever it was the dentist injected.'

Best smiled quietly.

I said, 'I would like to think that it was an act. It would fit into the picture I have in mind of Yeats. But the injection gives him the benefit of the doubt.'

'Yes,' Best agreed. 'I can see Yeats resigned to being locked up in a bedroom as if it were all a part of some mystical ceremony connected with the operation: docile in the hands of the dentist.'

Before Mrs. Best I could not discuss the Steinbach operation to which later Yeats 'resigned' himself without consulting anyone. The talk took a turn again to George Moore.

'By the way,' I said, 'I have a little bit of history which may serve to dispel the legend of George Moore which Susan Mitchell circulated. You know?'

'Some men kiss and tell. Some men kiss and do not tell. But Moore tells and does not kiss.'

'Yes,' I said. 'But in the light of what I have heard, all that stuff about Moore's impotence is nonsense and Susan. A lady who knew him intimately told how Moore talked with a friend a few days before her marriage. Moore said:

'"You are to be married on Wednesday? This is Friday."

'"Yes."

'"Once married, you cannot be unfaithful to your husband."

'"Of course not. What makes you think of such a thing?"

'"Because your only chance of being unfaithful is *now*."

'So that was the beginning of *The Lovers of Orelay*. And you know the rest. Her name was . . . but she is married now; and as for Orelay, there is no such place. Where the lovers met was at Avignon. I was there, and the hotel proprietor offered to show us the bedroom of the Lovers of Orelay. He was quite intrigued.

'When Moore published the story, his friend called on him. She was indignant; and she swore that she would never speak to him again.

'"When you need me," Moore said, characteristically ignoring her statement, "hum a bar of Chopin's *Tannenbaum.*"

'Years after, when Moore was ill in Lady Carnarvon's Nursing Home, a stately figure dressed in black came out of his room and disappeared. George lay on his bed, which was covered with roses, and his face wore an ecstatic look. I spoke to him, and he said as one in a daze, "I have been in Paradise. I just heard a bar of *Tannenbaum*".'

Still on the subject of Moore, I remarked that Moore was more revolted by the thought of old age than by death. He had resigned his somewhat unresignable nature to the inevitability of the latter. He refused to let the thought of it enter his mind, whereas the decay of a tooth, the greying of the hair—signs of age—repelled him. I tried to tell him how Epicurus, in his endeavour to rid men of the fear of death, said, 'While I am, death is not. When death is, I am not.' In other words, the two never meet. But Moore dismissed the subject impatiently. He hated contemplation. As for me, there is but little consolation in the Epicurean subtilty, for it's the dying that hurts.

'*Malheureusement, pour être mort, il faut mourir,*' Best added. 'Ah, there's the rub! Obviously, the best fate is to get out before you know what hit you. That is what Julius Cæsar is said to have preferred, if you believe the story that, when asked what kind of death he would choose, he answered, "A sudden one." And didn't he get it? He surely did. He lived by the sword and died by many daggers. There's something in a man's death that becomes his life, some connection between a man's greatness and the manner of his death. Who wants to die "a straw death", as the Irish called death in bed? Cæsar spent a great soul as became him: unperturbed by pain, he rebuked his faithless friend. Who could live up to him? In Shakespeare's case there was still another "rub". He was afraid that, bad as Life is, there may be something worse behind it. Awful thought! And one rendered all the more ominous because it was entertained by, so far as we know, one of the greatest intellects of all time. It is an uncomfortable thought with which to fascinate the mind, if we forget that the mind comes after birth and has as little to do with Life as the perfume, imperishable as it is, has to do with the fate of the rose-bush. The thought that if we became "abject from the spheres", as my friend the poet, Watson, phrased it, " there may be nothing to stop our fall ". There is something to be said for the theory that if we have left our Golden Age behind us, we are unlikely to be steering for another Age of Gold. We may be on the downward grade *en masse*, for all we know. So let us not take a look at history, lest we think that there may be something worse coming to us and nothing to stop our decline and fall.

> 'Ay! but to die, and go we know not where;
> To lie in cold obstruction and to rot . . .
> To bathe in fiery floods, or to reside
> In thrilling region of thick-ribbed ice;
> To be imprisoned in the viewless winds,
> And blown with restless violence round about
> The pendant world: or to be worse than worst
> Of those that lawless and uncertain thoughts
> Imagine howling: 'tis too horrible!
> The weariest and most loathed worldly life
> That age, ache, penury and imprisonment
> Can lay on Nature is a paradise
> To what we fear of death.'

'Lawless and uncertain!' The Master of the Adjective!

'Shakespeare must have had a greater fear of death than anyone who is known to us, greater than Oliver Cromwell's, who feared it rightly, since he believed in eternal punishment; worse than Dr. Johnson's, for Shakespeare had a mightier and intenser imagination than either. Goethe did not take it quite so badly. In one of his exuberant moments he assured himself that, " Death cannot be an evil because it is universal." But so is disease, and disease manages to be quite an evil universally. The best we can say for ourselves is that, for better or for worse (like marriage), we are all in the same boat. Perhaps that's what Goethe meant. I'm a poor philosopher. You need to be celibate to philosophise.

' Seeing that this is so, there is a lot to be said for the Friendly Brothers who remain friendly in the boat. That is why they limit and select the passengers: bores can put up with each other better than geniuses.

' My consolation is that all my forebears died; and I cannot be worse off than they are—provided we do not meet. After all, death is nothing unusual.

' Isolation and perpetual loneliness, the loneliness of an elemental, I admit would be hard to bear; but, then, one would have to be immortal to put up with it; but, seeing that gregariousness is a part of the make-up of human nature, such a fate would be outside the terms of reference, so to speak.

' Death has not got us yet, so what about using it meantime to enhance life? To me death is the turpentine in the athletes' liniment: it keeps the muscles tense. And though you can imagine life without it, it would be an unsustainable bore. In the present scheme of things, Life is quite impracticable without its scavenger.'

I was homilising too much, so I asked suddenly, ' Have you ever kept a list of the seventy-six corrections you sent George Moore? '

Best was George Moore's proof-reader, grammarian and literary adviser.

Best smiled. He thought little of his appointment as corrector of George Moore's grammar and syntax. Moore employed Atkinson and W. K. Magee as well as Best. You might think that he was one of these modern authors who are hardly more than editors of other people's brains. But Moore was more than that: he had words at his command. He could extenuate a story and, above all, he had a sense of style. Smoothness was its characteristic.

Now both smoothness and sequence are gone from the novel. The Subjective or Stream of Consciousness has been substituted. And the Subjective covers a multitude of sins. The so-called ' modern ' novel appears to me to be a garbage-pail or ash-can which contains any or every cast-off remnant of living: old clothes, broken crockery, back numbers, stale food and decaying fish. I might have guessed that there was Chaos coming, for Joyce had his aerilon out and caught rumblings from Rimbaud, rumours of a revolt that cast its shadow before the revolution, and was destined to turn things topsy-turvy until hideousness took the place of beauty, and slavery the place of liberty, and discord the place of harmony, disruption the place of unity—unless the cohesion that the galvanised garbage-pail gives to its contents be considered an unity: the bucket in this instance being the Subconscious. Naturally, these ' moderns ' in their obscurity were left to talk to themselves for the want of an audience. Joyce went one farther, and talked to himself in his sleep: hence *Finnegans Wake*.

The time is more or less ripe: it is the age of cross-word puzzles, anthologies, detective stories and relative education; America hailed this Babel from the Berlitz schools of Europe. . . .

' Americans are all detectives,' Best asserted. ' They love something that provides scope for detective work. The stupendous associations in *Finnegans Wake* must be a godsend to detectives. Particularly those who knew neither Dublin nor Joyce.'

I concurred.

' You and I would be anathema to the authorities on Joyce, because we knew him. Somebody sent me a book on Joyce and Dublin lately, written by some professor at an American college—don't forget that Æ said that you must be always on the look out for the specialist in America—with a photograph of the author. This showed a full-faced, compact-headed, alert young man. The painstaking thoroughness of his investigation was astonishing. He had consulted every street directory of Dublin of the period. He took as real, characters which were composite or mere figments of Joyce's imagination. He actually gave their addresses. Detective work, as you say; but it reminded me of the Hollywood mortician who came over to measure Annie Laurie's chapel. The pity of it is that so much research and intelligence should be devoted to European will-o'-the-wisps and turned away from America, which is an inexhaustible source of inspiration.'

'Forms more real than living man,' Best quoted.

'Exactly,' I said. 'And therefore all the less vacuous.'

An investigator would be shocked to realise from our talk how little of a prophet Joyce appears to his own countrymen.

Then I remembered the denunciatory poem printed on what resembled a galley-sheet that Joyce shot back at us from Flushing when he arrived in Holland. Printed abroad it was, as the quotation marks beneath and not above words showed.

'Surely you were not exempted from his indignation? You must have been included in *The Holy Office*, rhymed pentameters on a galley sheet?' I asked.

'It was *Gas from a Burner* that was on a galley sheet. *The Holy Office* was in two columns instead of the one column of *Gas from a Burner*.'

'That's the one I got. It was burned with my

house. What did you do with yours?' I asked eagerly.

'I tore it up,' said Best.

'I was a recipient of *Gas from a Burner*, his invective against "Maunsell's publisher", who would not print *Dubliners* for fear of giving offence to the King.'

'Was it offensive?'

'Not at all. Joyce wrote to the King. His secretary wrote back saying that His Majesty took no interest in such matters. Both letters are published in the Preface to *Dubliners*. The publisher was pilloried in *Gas from a Burner*, and the rest of us in the first epistle, the one I am looking for. Magee was derided as one who would not

"His hat unfix
Either to pint or crucifix."

I was

"One whose conduct seems to own
A preference for a man of tone."

The man of tone was Trench, whom he called "Haines" in *Ulysses*. I wish I could find my copy now, but it was destroyed by the bandits who burned my house.'

'I tore up my copy,' repeated Best.

And then our interest turned to Best's pictures, of which he had a nice collection of the best-known Irish artists, from Nathaniel Home to Jack Yeats.

We went upstairs to inspect the pictures. I can recognise a Hone anywhere; and a Jack Yeats. I am not so sure of the others, for my knowledge of painting is almost as wanting as my knowledge of music. I much prefer to see an armchair in a room than a piano.

'This is my Abigail Mosser,' Best said, 'and it is one of the finest of my pictures.'

That I could see. The drawing was exquisite, particularly the drawing of the eyelids of the girl, some French sitter she found in Paris.

'She painted a lot of portraits: everybody of her time, and that was pretty long. She must have been ninety-six when she died. She used to say, "Let me sit with my back to the light so that I may pass for ninety-three." She might be still living, but that she foresaw an increase in succession duty. She offered to paint me. I refused.'

'Why?' asked Best.

'One thing deterred me. Some of her sitters came to a bad end—hanging and that sort of thing. Take the case of Sir Roger Casement. She painted him, and what happened. . . ?'

But my remarks were out of keeping with the tone of that peaceful house.

It was nearly eleven o'clock when we parted. The evening was still an evening. Darkness had not come on to bring with it night. I turned to the left by the canal and passed the lock gate off which Professor Reynolds fell and saved himself by anticipating the superfluous summons to 'Hauld on!' from the jarvies on the bridge.

The lock gates were not more worn than they were thirty years ago. There were no more rope rings cut into the wooden bollards, and the long handles of the gates were still sound enough to take your weight when you sat on them. Through one of the sluices the water rushed in a white cascade. How blessed is Dublin in its waterways and its silences, through which you can hear the noise of rural water! And how happy it is in that interesting people live within easy reach of one another to the traveller on foot!

Thinking thus, I returned home and to bed.

CHAPTER TEN

The Dublin–Galway Train

IT'S A GREAT thing to catch a train!

There are few running in Ireland now compared to what there were before we won our freedom, in which freedom, freedom from easy transport was apparently included. But enough of that! Here I am in the ten-fifteen bound for Galway, the capital of one of the Four Provinces, Connaught. I take care to choose a seat by the window on the right facing the engine, because that will give me a view of the now-disused Royal Canal. The railway company bought it up to avail itself of its levels, so now it lies free from the slow barges that used to be drawn by a mule with trailing rope, a long avenue of water lined by old elms.

For the first few miles I will be like one of those Chinese travellers who never write of the incidents or the inconveniences of their journeys; and they must have been much more irksome there than here.

I will not look out of the window at the dome of the Custom House when we are crossing the Liffey, because I will be travelling on the Loop Line bridge; and I do not want the old anger I felt at the men who permitted the city to be defaced by that eyesore to arise again. There won't be a word out of me until we reach Clonsilla, where the canal comes into view. We will pass by many a village with a lovely Gaelic name just like the one I have just mentioned, Clonsilla, The Meadow of the Willow Trees. Whoever lived in it is forgotten. Only the memory of his cell remains.

'Where are you going, sir?'

'Cootehill,' I replied unthinkingly.

The ticket collector stood in the doorway with something shining metallically half hidden in his right hand. He looked at me quizzically, then laughed.

'First stop, Liffey Junction,' as I extended my ticket. 'His nibs the stationmaster told me to take care of you.' He jerked his head over his shoulder. Much to my relief, he smiled. A breezy, good-natured fellow.

'Tell him you did take care of me. Do you expect a full train?'

'There's days they come and days they go. What moves them there's no tellin'; an excursion, maybe. But then again I've seen her half empty during an excursion. There's one thing certain: there's more going than coming.'

'Emigration to England?' I suggested.

'And why wouldn't they go? Good wages; and they don't have to be in before dark.'

'But if this emigration goes on, what will become of the Irish Nation?' I asked anxiously.

'I wouldn't mind that. There's plenty of English coming in; we are just exchanging populations.'

And a good thing, too, I reflected.

He turned my ticket upside down. After a careful scrutiny he punched it, then continued light-heartedly with a sigh:

'Never fear! They'll come back here to die. Ireland's a great burial-ground.'

Two young men with shining faces and Roman collars made of rubber came into the carriage, not emigrants they, but immigrants to the great theological college called Maynooth, by the side of the Royal Canal. They took seats beside each other, and one of them handed the collector tickets for two. He punched them reverently. Another pair of clergymen arrived; with them a broad-faced lieutenant of the U.S. Navy. He had brown eyes widely separated over full, sunburnt cheeks that told of sun on the Pacific. It took the three some time to settle. At last they were seated with the lieutenant between them. They gazed at the two students, and their smiles died away.

The shouts outside ceased. We started. Silence

settled on the compartment. Behind my magazines I tried to discover what was the 'deep determinant' that made me mention 'Cootehill'. One of the priests produced a little book, changed over and sat beside me, and began to move his lips.

I retreated into the Subconscious as the train crossed the Liffey. Soon steep walls confined us: we were passing along the deep cut by Whitworth Road. Above our heads on the left was Mountjoy Gaol and the Royal Canal. Soon I saw a large round tower built of cut stone. It was much larger than any other round tower in the land, a copy, revealing, in spite of its size, the poverty of imagination in those who planned it to mark the tomb of Daniel O'Connell, the Emancipator and founder of the cemetery. Innovations were the cut stones and the surmounting cross: Glasnevin Cemetery, a great burial-ground!

If extension in size alone were to be taken as a sign of originality, surely that mild looney, Endymion, must be handed the palm for his invention of an ocean liner three thousand miles long; but they have not yet build one to cross the Atlantic instantaneously. The tallest round tower in the country takes its place to shorten Dan O'Connell's passage to Heaven.

At last the long water began.

Mile after mile the train went on. A lock appeared, a very deep lock, 'The Deep Sinking', the last, perhaps, before the long level across the centre of the country. Beside it stood the cottage of the lock-keeper, to whom life must be leisurely now, as by day he waits for barges that never come, and by night lies listening to the sound of water pouring over the gates or flowing through one of the open sluices. I wondered what lore is his: what tells him to open a sluice in the gate or when to let the water overflow; and what tales he tells to magnify the canal and increase his own importance. It would take a good shanachie to give significance to it now.

His wife came to the door with a cloth in her hand. Three bare-legged children with morning faces dodged past her skirts and lined up to salute the train, the train that had deprived the canal of any business and had given their parents long leisure to dally and produce. Strange, is it not, that out of idleness comes the greatest feat of creation in the world? So the children stood and saluted the compensating train, that, though it took many adults away, yet enabled those who were left to make up for their loss.

What a pleasant sight is a white-washed cottage with its roof of warm thatch; with its half door, little windows and deep eaves! How restful is the spell of it! How he who is borne past it longs to stop and remain! The outside has such allure that the pilgrim never thinks of the darkness within and the cramped space. So, too, it is with a yacht. The *Shamrock* showed her emerald hull and her gleaming copper keep as she cut the azure water, heeling over on a tack. White as the wing of a turning gull, her lofty wing of canvas spread: lovelier without than on deck, where all is bustling and alert; and where the canvas is more a concern than a joy forever. What constitutes the spell of a cottage nestling in the folds of the hills or standing by the long and lonely canal? Nothing but the promise of something stable in the flux, some straw to catch at as we hurtle on.

The more you regard the things outside, the less you become conscious of your journey. The moving panorama occupies your mind: so much so that you do not notice your passage until the terminus is reached. On the other hand, if you do not look out of the window, but fix your attention only on that which is in the carriage, you are not conscious of movement at all.

There are places on this earth where time seems to be speeded up and to pass more quickly than in others. One of these places is the city of New York, where the moon appears to take a week only to slide through all its phases. Other places there are; one of them is Ireland, where from crescent to full and to crescent again it takes a lunar month. Therefore life seems longer in Ireland than in America, though the proportion of centenarians is almost the same in either country. In America even a toothache would be welcome to arrest you and to make you think of your own individuality, to hold you for a moment in the swirl. There are more stabilisers than toothaches in Ireland: two of them were with me in the train. They teach that man should turn his thoughts inwardly and contemplate eternity, which is the cessation of motion, and so save himself from the transience of time. I get somewhat the same results by gazing at the long canal that is always the same: one unchanging length of lilied water, no matter where you are.

This must be the reason why my Subconscious always chooses a seat on the right in my journey to the West.

But what will explain the recurring vision that comes to me more than once or twice within a season of a pool of water crystal clear, at the bottom of which a little fish lies over the sand with his fins moving transparently, while beyond the pool a tiny waterfall trickles? I know, of course, that this, in the view of the psychologists or psychiatrists, is very significant and very ominous. To them water is a symbol of the most discreditable significance. . . . Water is more than the symbol of Time made manifest. Oh, no. It is something far more compromising—something *endo-psychic*, in fact.

Whatever it stands for, the long canal of pellucid water takes its place now.

Over the Plain of Nooth white clouds spread wide and high. The two young men in the rubber collars rose and, awkward with embarrassment, begged leave to be excused while they reached over the other passengers' heads for their modest luggage. With an inarticulate murmur they withdrew.

Immediately the priest nearest to me became voluble and said to the naval lieutenant, opposite to him, 'I heard a good one at Father Caffrey's last night.'

The priest beside him nudged the abstracted lieutenant to listen.

The lieutenant came to life and asked, 'When do we come to Mullingar?'

His companion, pointing to the priest beside me, said, 'Father Paddy has a good one for you.'

This brought the lieutenant to attention.

'Spill it,' he said.

The narrator drew a silken ribbon down his book to mark the page and said, 'Father Caffrey—but it would be a bit before your time—told us of two old women having an argument during the Eucharistic Congress which was held in Dublin. It seems that the poor people—and they're full of devotion, God be praised—were vying with each other as to who would have the best decorations in their windows to celebrate the Congress. One woman, we'll call her Mrs. Durkin, was showing no decorations at all. She was beginning to be the talk of the neighbours—she lived in Upper Dominick Street: you wouldn't know it. It's one of the poorer parts of Dublin. You might call it one of the slums. It's falling into decay, anyhow. Well, at long last, late one evening, what do two of her old cronies see but a picture—they were all hanging out holy pictures—a picture leaning out of Mrs. Durkin's top front. The two old ones on the street below looked at one another and then took another look at Mrs. Durkin's picture. After a good gaze, Mrs. Kennedy, we'll call her, says to her companion, Mrs. Cassidy:

' "It's St. Joseph, be Jingo." Only it wasn't "be Jingo"; but, now mind you, they mean no harm by it—but the Holy Name. "It's St. Joseph! be all that's holy," says she.

' Mrs. Cassidy has a good squint.

' "That's no St. Joseph," says she. "St. Joseph has a trim beard—but St. Patrick. I know him as well as Cassidy himself."

' "Ye must be losing yer sight, Mrs. Cassidy. It can't be St. Patrick, for St. Patrick's beard goes down to his belt," says Mrs. Kennedy.

' So they argued and argued, and were beginning to fight, when who comes out but Durkin from one of the licensed premises, that's what we call a saloon

—and they turned to him and one says, " Mr. Durkin," she says, " Mrs. Cassidy and me were wondering who the saint is in your wife's holy picture up there in the top front. I says it's St. Joseph. She says it's St. Patrick."

' " It's neither," shouts Durkin, waving his fists. " But a better man than either. That's Charles Stewart Parnell ! " '

It was perhaps too topical for the naval man. He smiled vaguely, but that was undoubtedly due to the fact that Fr. Paddy had raised his voice to a pitch of indignation when imitating Mr. Durkin's challenging assertion.

' I didn't get to bed until after four this morning,' he remarked. ' You would think that if it takes six hours for a hundred miles, it would pay the Company to put a restaurant car on the train.'

' We'll be at Mullingar in no time,' Fr. Paddy assured him.

The lieutenant turned his wrist and looked at his watch. He closed his eyes.

' Hold it now and listen to this.'

His companion beside him said, ' There was a fellow from a parish not a thousand miles from here who met a girl in London and married her in a registry office. His sister got to hear of it, and she was indignant at an unreligious marriage like that: and why shouldn't she? He came over here with the young lady, and they stopped in a hotel in Galway: wait till you come to Galway, and you'll never want to go anywhere else. His brother started to call on them, and he said as much to the sister. The idea didn't appeal to her at all; but seeing that her brother had made up his mind, at last she says, "If you must go, on no account let on you know that the woman he's living with is his wife."'

The lieutenant went blank.

Fr. Paddy explained, 'That's the way they look on it here.'

At last the train stopped. The 'Square Mill'—in another word, 'Mullingar'—had at last been reached. Many doors flew open, and a crowd rushed back towards the railway refreshment-room. In a moment there was a crowd four deep in front of the bar. Tea was handed out in containers. Bottles of Guinness reached those on the platform who could not fit themselves into the huddle in front of the bar.

There would be fourteen minutes for no apparent reason unless to give the passengers time to refresh themselves at a counter far too short to accommodate the occupants of one coach. The lieutenant emerged from the refreshment-room and was directed to a door marked 'Fir'. The translation underneath read, 'Gentlemen'. 'Ladies' was in English. Could it be that there was no equivalent for 'Ladies' in Gaelic?

I was still protected by my Subconscious when he returned. He smiled all around him. As the train started he took his seat with increasing smiles.

The cement wall enclosing the disused track for horse- and dog-racing was slowly receding. It caught the lieutenant's undimmed eyes. It reminded him of something he was trying to recall. The clergyman beside me opened his breviary. Silence settled only to be broken by the lieutenant saying:

'I got something in the Dolphin last night. But it wouldn't be in your line, as you don't play horses; besides, it's not until the Derby the year after this; and who knows where I'll be then? It's a tip about a yearling owned by—I don't know Irish, so I can't remember the name; but the owner appears to be the leader of the local Brains Trust. I wish I had written both names down. The horse is Pat, Pat something; but what's the use?'

Evidently there was none.

Fields in need of drainage spread on both sides. Here and there a substantial house of stone appeared. The reverend gentleman beside me closed his breviary and borrowed one of my magazines. At Moate the train stopped, but no doors were opened.

'Moate?' the lieutenant inquired.

The man beside him said:

'There's a great tumulus here—one of the biggest

in the country. From it the town takes its name. In Ireland they call all the tumuli " moats ".'

'Is there a moat around them?'

'Oh, no.'

'Then why are they called moats?'

No answer.

The second clergyman said:

'They get their name probably from the Norman word " motte ", meaning a mound. There are many words of Norman French derivation that have passed into the language. The Normans were there longer than is realised. There are some of them here still; that is, their names—family names—are here. They are " more Irish than the Irish themselves ", as the saying is. Your own name is an example. " Burke " was once " de Burgho ".'

The lieutenant was all alert.

So his name is 'Burke'.

The expanse of the River Shannon shone as we crossed it hard by Athlone, the Ford of Luan. The hydro-electric installation on the river was compared unfavourably with the harnessing of Niagara. The politics that made it a failure on the Canadian side and a success on the American were expounded. The lieutenant saw that the magnitude of the work was too much for his audience, who did not like the Shannon to take a second place to any river, seeing that it was bigger than any river in England.

After relapsing into silence for some minutes, he enquired:

'Is there a refreshment-room at Athenry?'

Neither of the reverend gentlemen could say. But one congratulated the naval man on the way he could remember a map. Another pause, and one of them said (the 'refreshment-room' must have reminded him):

'You were telling of that fellow with a hang-over in Boston. Well, here's one of a fellow who goes into an Irish pub. He was in a shocking condition.

'"For God's sake give me a cure," he calls to the barman.

'"D'ye think this is Lourdes?" the barman asks, after one look at him.'

The lieutenant's smile was puzzled.

'Nothing short of a miracle would have been any use to him,' Fr. Paddy explained.

But at Athenry, the Ford of the Kings, the refreshment-room—if you could believe the guard—was over the bridge at the other side of the station; and there was only a minute's wait.

My seat was getting so hot and irksome that it ousted my Subconscious, which was motivated by the pressure of my body on the seat. Just in time!

'More and more,' I found myself repeating as I looked at the great square castle of Oranmore.

I left Dublin to recover my peace of mind only to

find that the relaxation or suppression of the influences of the will which had inhibited my stream result in this suspicious word-association. Can't I even relax in a railway carriage but I must be pursued by endo-psychic existence?

There is not the least doubt about it, I am fast becoming a case for Al Robitesk, Mayer, Wundt or Ferenczi. And to think of it: there is not yet a doctor in Galway with a name alien enough to be alienist enough for me! When they hear what an opening there is for them they will all slip into a country where any of them may wind up by becoming Prime Minister. Sean Robitesk, Seumas Mayer or Eamonn Wundt. All they require is an Irish-given name. No prophet in Ireland is a countryman.

Was it because I had sat on my Subconscious so long that I was compelled to say 'More and more' for Oranmore? If so, what are the complicated psychic influences that compelled me to say it? 'Oranmore: more and more!' I see it all now. I have found myself out: I have been liberated from the Subconscious by the Conscious. I may be going a bit bats. But where's Stekel? Where's Hitschman? Where's Bleuler? There's only Dr. Bob MacLaverty in Galway who can explain and sublimate my mistake about Oranmore; and he's Professor of Obstetrics to the University, and that makes me feel all the more shy. Anyway, there's nothing for it but to confess to him that a young lady of my acquaintance has bought Oranmore Castle and is doing it up with power, light, hot and cold water and all modern conveniences; more and more! If the doctor will permit me, I will call on the lady to see how she is getting on in Oranmore.

I heard someone saying to the lieutenant: 'Yes, this is Galway. And why would you want to go farther? Why should anyone want to go farther? There is no farther to go.'

CHAPTER ELEVEN

The Citie of the Tribes

WHY SHOULD ANYONE want to go farther than Galway? Why indeed?

Galway is the gossip capital of Ireland. It is not without significance that the statue in its principal Square should be that of a shanachie or story-teller. The citizens know (sometimes beforehand) what is happening in every county, and lack of information neither limits nor diminishes the tale. Therefore it came as no surprise to me to learn that I was expected. It used to surprise me to hear that I was welcome until I realised that that was but a figure of speech, an exordium indispensable to conversation.

You do not altogether leave Dublin by crossing the island to its western side, but you leave a great deal of bitterness and acrimony behind. Personalities take the place of politics in Galway. The first citizen of Galway was Morty Mor—Big Martin—who died a little while ago. Never did the Gaelic language record a death more majestically in three fateful words,

MORTY MOR MORB.

It had the language of Rome behind it, in which each word can fall like a stroke of fate. It is not as unbecoming as it would seem to talk of a dead man in a town where there are so many living persons about, because in Galway, as in China, the dead are more important than the living, so that a friendly reminiscence is enough to recall them from oblivion.

Morty Mor McDonough was big-headed and very tall. He dressed in black, for, since clergymen wear it, black commands respect; and as the greatest employer in the town, respect was his due. His character was as great as his power: he could talk up to the other men in black, and there was no cowing him. His rheumy eyes gazed slowly at you as he made up his mind. He was loyal to Galway town, the City of the Tribes, so loyal that he resented the visit of two missioners from Meath who came to collect for what they called the Maynooth Mission to China. They were astonished to find themselves refused. Conscious of power, they became insistent and brusque. Morty Mor spoke.

'I will not subscribe to a Maynooth Mission to China; but *I will subscribe* to a Chinese Mission to Maynooth to teach you manners.'

It was a new conception: a Chinese Mission to the great theological college of Maynooth or to anywhere at all! The Chinese do not send missions to proselytise 'foreign devils'. That is why it came as an original suggestion from Morty Mor. Suppose that the suggestion were to be adopted. How wonderful it would be if a sampan from China were to berth in the Liffey and its cargo of bonzes to come ashore and to proceed in a barge up the quiet waters of the Royal Canal to Maynooth! If they were not first subjected to a reception by the President and an urine analysis, their progress would be one serene procession in their reconditioned barge or house-boat. With what dignity would they acknowledge the salutations of the aborigines who would wave them on with cheers of encouragement on their unprecedented journey. With what gravity would they await, with hands hidden in their robes, the inrush of water that would raise them up to higher levels in the locks until, at last, the mule, garlanded and with harness decorated, would draw them westward through the long reach to the wall of Maynooth. How they would admire that wall, impassively comparing it with the wall of the Forbidden City that held the Old Buddha before the rising of the Boxers undid her. And then the reception in the *aula maxima* in Maynooth: yellow and purple; bonze, bishop and acolytes in one glory of double imperial dyes; the Imperial yellow of the Middle Empire and the purple of Imperial Rome!

Those introductions:

'T'as Yuan Ming from the Temple of the Haunted

Dragon by the Peak of the Celestial Pool meet Dr. Cod, Bishop of Ferns.' 'Ma Tu Fang from the Pavilion of Shining Truth by the River of White Jade—Dr. Scanlan.' (Afar off, voices singing, 'Hurry to bless the hands that play.')

It was so convincing, albeit a vision, that I began to detect a Chinese influence in the deportment of the Galway divines: a sedateness and weight, an *embonpoint* and amplitude, that endowed them with a ceremonious courtesy that had something in it of the Middle Kingdom.

I did not come to Galway to dream of China; and far be it from me to teach manners or anything else. I will turn my face to the South when the time comes, comforted by the thought that I never had a pupil.

What a town Galway is, beside its rippling, abundant river, swan-laden, salmon-full! The Corrib must be one of the largest rivers in the world for its length, which cannot be more than a mile or two. It used to turn many a mill. Its canalised waterways are there to-day, green-haired with weeds and overgrown; but as crystal clear as when they first rushed to the sea from Lough Corrib and Lough Mask.

If the mayor had any taste he would cut the weeds from the river-banks and let even wild roses, that ask for no gardener, take their place; and he would strictly forbid plastering with cement the faces of houses that owe their proportions to the influence of

Spain, houses of cut stone that had large, oblong windows centuries before England emerged from half-timbered, casement-lit cottages. The few remains of historical houses owe their preservation to a priest who cherished history in stone. Now the stones are painted over and any travelling circus can hire Eyre Square.

All my wishes are fulfilled; but if I had one more wish it would be that I might be mayor of Galway even for one year—Galway, a cleaner Venice, with living water in place of the brackish, stagnant canals! The men who built those Galway houses with gardens giving on the mill-races felt the beauty that water has and its power to inspire. The sides of the mill-races now are filled with whatever rubbish lies out of reach of the stream. You need not be a landscape-gardener to see what a town of enchantment Galway could be made were its many water-courses to be lined with lilac, laburnum, woodbine and hawthorn; especially hawthorn, which is exempt from vandalism because it is unlucky to bring it into a house. These bushes would cost nothing or next to nothing to plant; and they would have a double bloom in the long Spring, a bloom above and a bloom reflected. The streets are clean; why should the banks of the clear streams be left as witnesses to the tolerance for ruin which seems to lie in the character of the Irish nowadays?

What has obsessed the Irishman with thanatophilia—this love of death, decadence and decay? The toleration of eyesores is its outward sign. Even the farmer, when he has prospered and moves to a larger house, leaves the old sheiling to rot and deface the landscape with its gable angles rising against the sky.

Spanish Arch must have been the sea-gate of Galway town. It abuts the river. Beyond it lies nothing but a few nondescript cottages and the empty dock. Its watch-tower is half gone, but the arch and one closed-up beside it are still strong.

So Clare Sheridan, the sculptor, has bought both the arch and the houses next to it. She plans to have a hanging garden on the top of the arch overlooking the rushing water. Her niece, Shane Leslie's only daughter, Anita, is restoring, not far away, the strong castle of Oranmore, the fortress that guarded the approach by 'the Great Shore' to Galway from the south.

This is not the first of the old XIVth-century castles to be rescued from utter dilapidation in Galway. Yeats restored the castle at Ballylee close to Coole Park. He called his keep Thor Ballylee, because he thought that 'castle' was somewhat ostentatious, although every large dwelling of stone built in Ireland before Cromwell came with his bible and his Black and Tans was called a castle.

Yeats was well aware of this toleration of ruin in the heart of the native. He knew that they would preserve nothing if left to themselves. He knew that out of their perpetual preoccupation with the past came a desire to make all grandeur portion and parcel of that Past. Therefore he composed the lines to be engraved on a stone of the door of his tower, praying,

> 'May these characters remain
> When all is ruin once again.'

So why all this pother about ornamenting a town? The answer is obvious. In it lies the difference between beauty and ugliness, between grandeur and meanness, between cleanliness and dirt. A beautiful place engenders sentiments of pride and affection in the hearts of those who inhabit it. This gives rise to stability and to patriotism. Conversely, they who dwell in squalor, deprived of beauty, have nothing in their souls but a reflex of that squalor, discontent and hatred for all things lovely and pleasant. In this tragedy lies, and the road to rebellion until Squalor sits enthroned: all this in Ireland, the wealthiest country in the world.

Into Oranmore Castle builders are bringing baths and basins and hot and cold water. Electric power and light are already laid on. Great cisterns collect water from the slightly domed roof. Walls are being plastered and panelled. Even the dungeon or prison on the third floor which took a small boy weeks to clear of rubbish, in which a baby's skeleton was found, is being repaired.

Maybe this and other restorations are the result of the scarcity of houses. Whatever be the cause, it is something to be grateful for that people of taste are giving an example of what can be done in a town that has the enviable endowment of ancient walls and waters running beneath them—everything for its inhabitants but the eye to see.

I took tea with some friends. I soon discovered that there was much that I had missed in Galway. Apparently I had been thinking only of its natural advantages that could make it one of the loveliest towns on earth. Little did I realise that already it was a Cytherea, a shrine where Venus was worshipped. I thought that I knew the history of Galway. I had read Hardiman and studied the report of the Commissioners who were appointed to preserve its archives. But the enactments touching Venus only referred to fines for those citizens who permitted their houses to become houses of assignation for friars. It was all so long ago that I discounted it as accurate history. But though the friars who dealt in such real estate were long dead, from what I was now told I judged that the reign of an obscure Venus was flourishing still. At last I exclaimed:

'But if such things go on, how does society hold together in the daytime?'

I did not intend to expostulate or to appear incredulous. I merely wondered how such things could be kept clandestine in such a small town. I had often wondered how Anne Boleyn, Shakespeare, Mistress Fitton, Kit Marlowe, Ben and the rest of the boys 'got away with it', so to speak, where the houses were half-timbered and everyone knew the neighbour's business. The answer was now apparent: they didn't get away with anything. There were always intelligent observers about. So the beauty that I longed to see by the canals and river is hidden in the boudoirs of the town. It was a consolation in a way, but a way that was questionable.

While I was occupied with such thoughts as these, my hostess asked:

'Did you hear about the retreat for women?'

And I had been thinking that, by her account, their bedrooms were their retreats. But I was wrong! 'Retreat', in the sense in which the word was used, meant a religious meeting to hear sermons, to examine conscience, and to pray.

'I heard nothing about the Retreat.'

How could I? I was only just arrived.

'Oh, you must hear it. It was advertised for weeks: "*Women only*. On the 4th there will be a retreat for women; and sermons on the Sacrament of Matrimony".'

'Weren't all the men aching with curiosity to find out what the sermons would be like?'

She smiled complacently; then she went on:

'Well, the great day, or rather evening, came round at last. Every woman, including Mrs. Dunne, that could get out, was there to hear a Franciscan Father preaching. Now, Mrs. Dunne came from the Claddagh, and she had eight children, including ones that she was nursing, so it was no easy matter for her to leave the house. Anyway, she took the baby under her shawl and off with her to the Retreat. She was a bit late when she arrived and the sermon was in full blast. God help me! I shouldn't say that. But you know what I mean. The preacher had got himself worked up.'

The lady laughed so much at this point that my curiosity, inert for the most part about Retreats, was aroused. At last she was able to continue.

'Well, Mrs. Dunne got in and found a place by the door. She listened for a minute to the sermon on Holy Matrimony and then said fervently as she turned to go: "I wish to God I knew as little about it as that fellow".'

I thought of the white swans stemming the Corrib and waiting for a word from the Franciscans of comfort to the birds.

With such things to concern them indoors, is it any wonder that there is apathy among the citizens regarding the appearance of their town?

CHAPTER TWELVE

'Going West on my Journey'

THE JOLTING OF the crowded bus brought up fond memories of the Broadstone Railway Station in Dublin with its colonnade of Ionic pillars built high above the level town. If there had been no preceding architecture of the kind, the Broadstone Station would have been the loveliest building in the world, provided, of course, that no other contemporary building of similar design existed. The Broadstone is altered now, like many other good and stately things. It is a bus station. The excuse, of course, was economy and, of course, that inseparable carrot, efficiency. Look at the result: a sea-sick bus-full of disgruntled passengers, and the broken bridges and the ripped-up metals of the railway—uncertainty of travel and certainty of delay. You pay for first-class tickets abroad to end in the commune of a bus.

When the Athenians juggled the cash that the trusting Allies deposited in the island of Delos, Athens was beautified. The Parthenon was the result. Relatively a thousand times more money has poured into Dublin lately since the ruination of the railways than ever ancient Athens knew. The Hospital Sweep has brought in hundreds of millions, some of which are spent on hospitals, sanatoria, lunatic asylums and convalescent homes—buildings that have a hint of medical philanthropy—but not a red cent is spent on that which is as justifiably medical as the hospitals: prophylaxis against disease by means of slum-clearing and clean houses. It might be thought by some archæologist or historian, if such be found, to take sufficient interest in this trough between waves of culture, that the hospital was the thing, and not the cure.

Millions will not beautify Dublin, any more than the thousands subscribed did honour to O'Connell, simply because culture, good taste, has been scorned ‘ and great art beaten down ’. So better build a few dozen more sanatoria and coughing-stations to receive the casualties of the slums; but hands off the slums that produce such a prosperous harvest of hospitals without one colonnaded masterpiece among them all.

The bus jolted along. A woman beside me congratulated me on getting a seat. There were many people left behind. Would there be an auxiliary bus for them, or would they be left to stay the night in Galway town? She could not say; but I could, for I was forced, for the lack of bus accommodation not very long ago, to spend a night in the Railway Hotel. I was about to send a telegram to the President to put his Rolls Royce or whatever car he favours at the disposal of myself and half a dozen benighted travellers, until I cooled and consoled myself by the thought that a night in Galway, in spite of its early-to-bed proclivities, was not such a hardship. The Manager of the buses explained the shortage by the sale of one hundred buses to Northern Ireland. Another effort to 'bring in the North'? He thought that I was wrong when I suggested that it was the late Government's way of encouraging tourist traffic: 'Not an inch.' And years ago you could reach Dublin in five hours. Now it may take two days.

The names of the places to which the buses go are printed in Gaelic. Native speakers cannot read Gaelic, but they interpret it by interrogating the conductor or the driver.

A landscape drenched after rain spread to the right and left. I remarked to the man beside me, 'It's rather unseasonable weather for this time of year.'

'Sure, it isn't this time of year at all,' he announced.

Where else but in Connemara can you meet a man living in the Fourth Dimension and yet riding in a bus? He is travelling: so Space denies Time.

On the left one far-off conical hill broke the long

monotony. We passed a ruined castle or keep that stood solitary by the side of the road. It told of a lake or marshes that were drained, for it could not have defended any road now, so open was the ground. Stone walls demarking fields and drainage ditches were passed, proof of generations of toiling men who worked to reclaim land, the yield of which their landlords enjoyed—sometimes. There were no landlords now; their places are taken by the Land Commission and the nameless legion of attorneys who own Ireland instead.

The ruins of Ross Abbey appeared on the left. Lough Corrib could not be far away, for the friars who built such abbeys loved the lakes or river which provided them with fish. Ross Abbey, with its square tower in the middle like that of Kilconnell near Aughrim, stood roofless. We were nearing Headfort, where the bus would stop and some of its occupants alight and relieve the congestion. The charm of Headfort consists in its being only seven miles from Cong. Bright-roofed, pleasant cottages cheered the scenery. There is little misery in the country; misery resides in the slums.

If there were no towns larger than Galway, there would be no slums. Galway has a population of nineteen thousand; and that is about the maximum a town should have. When the towns of the future are broken up and replaced by satellite villages to limit the devastating power of the weapons of modern war, there will be many Galways in the world. What a pleasant world that will be, although it will lack Galway's limpid streams.

I thought of the difficulty of moving crowded populations. The present system of emigration leaves too much nostalgia in the hearts of those removed. The solution is to remove self-contained portions of cities, for every city has villages within it such as the Chelseas of London and New York. People become homesick because their social life is uprooted: they miss the gossips of home. In other words, they miss the scandals of their home towns. Therefore, when founding a colony overseas, it is necessary to move the chatterboxes, the barbers and the dentists; for no man worth his salt will take his scandals vicariously on the movies and such-like substitutes.

Limpid streams! Was there ever a village more endowed with running water than the village of Cong? The name comes from the Gaelic 'Cunga', meaning a neck, for it is situated on the neck of land between the lakes of Mask and Corrib which a subterranean river joins. The Local Government Board, in the days when the British ran the country, cut a canal to enable boats to ply between the two large lakes.

The time came when the canal was finished and it

was ready to be 'opened' by the leading members of the Local Government and other philanthropists. The waters of Lough Mask rushed in—and disappeared! The region was limestone, and the waters went to join the subterranean river which had been formed æons ago by the action of the acidulated waters on the limestone. Even the water went underground as a protest against British domination in those days; and yet the British yoke was mild compared with the acid infiltration of some of those in office since. In the old days anyone with a friend in court could, by assiduous drinking, drink himself into the Local Government Board. Now everything is dry: canal and all. And Sir Henry Robinson, who preferred good manners to go-getting, is dead.

Grey mill walls diagonalled by ivy rise from placid waters overgrown by lilies and flowering water-plants. Broken weirs and sluices show where the mill-wheels were. Under leaning woods, the escaping streams run free. Woods! 'They haven't got rid of all the gentlemen yet.' Lord Ardilaun planted the woods when he built Ashford Castle at the head of Lough Corrib. He must have employed the same architect as did Michael Nugent.

Cong, with its caves and subterranean river and many fountains, is the site of the Abbey where the remains of Roderick O'Connor, the last King of

Ireland, rested for seven years until they were re-interred in Clonmacnoise. In Cong was the famous cross of Cong, a processional cross curiously wrought and marvellously designed. As an example of goldsmiths' craft it is one of the wonders of the world.

Into the bus an angler in the uniform of an angler came with his net and rod. Evidently he was an Englishman, because he was looking for someone with whom to talk. This is directly opposite to the accepted picture of the self-contained, tacit Englishman; but you should meet one on fishing bent in a foreign country such as Ireland where he is revered. Then he loosens himself in—sometimes, but not always—condescending speech. If we have accepted the exception he represents to the stage Englishman of the Dr. Livingstone legend, more's the pity that he cannot see that all Irishmen are not stage Irishmen derived from Cruikshank in the pages of *Punch*. And he should be the last to talk of dirt, seeing that the bath was introduced into England only after the return of the Anglo-Indians who took one as a refuge from the heat, whereas the so-called Turkish bath was well patronised in Dublin long before Warren Hastings was impeached. However!

Is there anything more annoying than the fatuous question, 'Do you believe in fairies?'—a question usually asked with a hint of condescension? What makes such a question obnoxious is the logic of the questioner and the imputation in the word 'belief' with all its undistributed meanings. Added to this, there is the deep conviction within you that all such matter-of-fact people are utterly incapable of understanding what the instinct is, or the gift whereby the water diviner, for instance, is enabled to find water, or the unsophisticated poet to reach the general heart, or the man or woman who is 'fey' to see fairies. This conviction causes you to resent such factual people; you feel a resistance and you sense a lack of sympathy. You know that they would catch a butterfly in a rat-trap or use a gauger's rod to sound the procreant omnipotence of the unconscious mind.

Such inquisitorial people are frequently found. They have only a limited time to hear an answer to their question and neither time nor attention to hear you out, if you are foolish enough to answer. Their minds are already made up, and they cannot get out of them.

My way of dealing with such a question is to retort with another question. When they repeat, 'Do you believe in fairies?' I ask, 'What, here?' I will admit that this is too disconcerting to be polite, for it is obvious that no fairy would appear in the bus that goes from Galway to Clifden the wrong way round.

From this it will be obvious that there is a time and a place for everything. Far from the mechanisms of this atomic age are the gay, mischievous and appeasable fairies, denizens of rath and hill.

Though they partake not of human food, they suffered from the potato famine when millions of those who had eyes to see and spells to placate them closed their famished eyes forever or turned them away from the mystic circles around the twisted thorn. The emigrant ship carried away many of those with whom they were in sympathy; mass schooling and regimented education shut the minds of the rest.

Darby Doolin could tell you that much better than I. It was he who told the father of Oscar Wilde, Sir William, what caused this defection.

'Troth, Sir, what betune them National Boards and Godless colleges, and other sorts of larnin', and the loss of the 'pratey, and the sickness, and all the people that's goin' to America, and the craturs that's forced to go to the workhouse, or is dyin' off in the ditches, and the clergy settin' their faces agin them, and tellin' the people not to *give in* to them, sarra wan of the Gintry will be found in the country, nor a word about them and their doin's in no time.'

Thus in beautiful musical speech was delivered an elegy on the fairies almost one hundred years ago.

But the fairies are immortal; they may withdraw, but they cannot be destroyed. They avoided commissioners, inspectors, school boards and examinations; survived the famine and the plague that followed it to carry off millions of their devotees, and withdrew into the Many Coloured Land amid the purple mountains and the reedy valleys of the West:

'The fairies, the whole pantheon of Irish demigods, are retiring one by one from the habitations of man to the distant islands where the wild waves of the Atlantic raise their foaming crests; or they have fled to the mountain passes and have taken up their abodes in those wild, romantic glens, lurking in the gorgeous yellow furze and purple heath amidst the savage, disrupted rocks or creeping beneath the warrior's grave.'

Well do I know where they are, for I have lived longer in Iol Daithe, Many Coloured Connemara, than Sir William Wilde. The wonder of this many coloured land lies in the change of colours, which are never for an hour the same shade. To name them in a language that has hardly a dozen names for colour would be impossible. Plum-blue, hyacinth, cyclamen and every flower that grows in the country would have to be enlisted, and then they would never give the impression of living and glowing hues. The mountain lakes are more than black; the mountains are lapis lazuli mixed with velvet brown; sea inlets take on shades that no words can name. . . .

'Have you ever caught a leprechaun (is that how you pronounce it?) behind a bush?'

I followed his gaze up a slope blazing with gorse in bloom.

'Which bush?' I asked, hoping to please him by showing that in Ireland there was at least one factual mind.

Instead of being grateful, he got out of the bus. He had intended to, anyway; but could there be a more alluring place to get out at than Cornamona, 'the turn of the Turf', Cornamona of the lovely name?

Casleen na Kirka—the Hen's Castle—was out to the left, standing on its solitary rock in an arm of Lough Corrib. The great lake was no longer to be seen. The castle's ruins are kept from falling by the late Lord Ardilaun's provision, for the castle has a history of its own. Some say that it got its name from an enchanted hen that laid an egg for every member of a garrison during a siege. Others—more factual, like me—say that Grace O'Malley, the sea queen of the West in the days when Queen Elizabeth reigned in England, came to her husband's rescue when he was locked up by his enemies in the castle. Her husband was called the Cock; and the castle was called after her who had raised its siege.

The bus was entering the Joyce Country. There was a rumour of old that every Joyce had six fingers on each hand and six toes on each foot, a tale that must have arisen as a corollary to the gigantic stature of that famous tribe.

The tumbling mountains that, when far away, were diamonded by flashes of rainy sunlight, are now close by, fit haunts of those 'immortal, mild, proud shadows' seen by men with enchanted eyes and by the artist, Jack Yeats, whose picture of 'The Others' is in my mind. His painting shows a countryman doubled with toil and hardship, leading a wretched donkey and cart along an exposed and endless road with one windswept tree beside it. Coming half from heaven and earth, 'The Others' may be seen clothed in dim gold, majestic, a vision which is the dream of the bowed man, his treasure and his sustenance: a splendour the very opposite of his lot. Here, where reedy pools and windy bogs have islanded a fair green knoll, 'The Others' have come down from their courts in the mountains which are richer than all earthly palaces. Only to those whose thoughts and feelings are intense enough to endow hill and glen with fitting splendour 'The Others' will appear. In this there is nothing that has not been known time out of mind.

> 'Democritus, the philosopher, writeth that we should pray we might ever see happy images and sights in the ayer, and that the good which

is meet and proper to our nature may rather come to us, than that which is evil and unfortunate . . . that there are good and bad images flying in the ayer which give a good or ill impression unto men, and incline men to vice or to virtue.'

The old biographer should have added that there are only certain places on earth proper to such images, for in certain places only may they be seen ' flying in the ayer '. If I am not already in such a place I soon shall be, for I am bound for a mountain-sheltered island in a lake not a mile from the Atlantic. Trees cover it, and it is ringed with the red-berried mystic rowan tree. There I will dwell actually as the poet Yeats dwelt in vision in Inisfree. Inisfree means Isle of Heather. The isle to which I am going is Frei-laun, Heather Island. ' Midnight's all a glimmer and noon a purple glow ' in both.

There I will abide with ' flying images ' for a month or two and seek their good impression before returning to the river rolling forever down the lea.

CHAPTER THIRTEEN

Freilaun

IN TULLY LAKE there is an island eleven acres in extent called 'Freilaun', which means Heather Island. It lies midway between the nearest shores under the great rock of Letter Hill, which shelters it from the prevailing western winds. The lake is shaped like a long oval which has been contracted near the middle where the island lies. On the eastern shore there is a garage which is also a boat-house. A boat is kept beside it by a little pier. A few minutes' rowing brings you to the island where the boat can run into a harbour the size of the boat. When you step ashore you are at the beginning of a path that winds crimson-walled by fuchsia, and roofed by laurel, rhododendrons and flowering shrubs. After thirty yards the air grows warmer because of a copse of linden and sycamore trees. Before you suddenly a long, two-storeyed, lime-white house comes into view with a veranda of brown timber running along over the first storey. Between the house and the lindens is a little court paved with irregular slats, russet and brown and sea-green. The silence that reigns in the island may be broken only by a startled blackbird or a belted bee barging back, by and large, from a foray on the spreading flowers; or, in the long Spring, by a cuckoo that sounds as if it were close by. At evening, a pair of wild pigeons make love-lorn moanings as they settle in the trees.

A bank behind the house rises as high and shelters it with trees and shrubs from any breezes from the North. To the south the view is open over the lake to the Twelve Bens of Connemara, which seem quite near, though glistening Diamond Mountain, the nearest of them, is five miles away.

On the ground floor every window gives on the green and purple of the rhododendrons or the pink of rambler roses crowding the garden wall. Over the lawn on the west side glimpses of the lake may be caught between the larger trees; but, though the house is in the middle of a lake, the lake-water is never heard lapping on the shore. It may be that the rowans, sallies and ivied trees that rim the lake keep away even the gentle sound of little waves.

Where the lake itself preserves the silence, it is needless to say that the ambrosial night is not made hideous by the brayings of a radio.

This is no place for the listless nor for the restlessness of youth; but a man well stepped on in years it suits well.

When I think that the poet Yeats spent a night on a rock beside Lough Gill gazing through the midnight glimmer at Inisfree, which he was never to reach to build his cabin, and of the years through which he longed in vain for his love, it is disturbing to know that the best poetry comes from a longing that must be forever unfulfilled. Yet here I am where I longed to be. All that I can do with my ease is to weave some light rhymes together about the passing away of comely things, and so sublimate my resentment against those who put buses in the place of the uncrowded trains.

There is plenty of tranquillity here in which to remember those nincompoops. I will see what will emerge. A few admonitory words, no more.

The comforting thing about poetry is that it requires no effort. It is one of the few things that will come if you leave it alone. So while the lines are murmuring in my ears, I will try to follow the path that goes round under the sheltering trees. Years ago, when the island was houseless but for the remains of a cottage, so undisturbed was it then that I came across a wild duck's nest with seventeen brown eggs. The wild duck nest no longer on the island; but on a smaller island to the south, called Half Moon Island, from its shape, there is an heronry. You can see the birds nesting on the tree-tops with their legs hanging down through their nests. I rowed past it yesterday and startled at least a dozen herons flapping out from the undergrowth. Though they are said to eat eight pounds of fish daily, I do not disturb them, for nothing good comes from upsetting the balance of Nature. Huntsmen are learning this far away in the Everglades, where they now spare the alligators, for these feed on snakes, not fish; and they not only keep the serpentine breed down, but they keep the ground moist in the arid summer.

The water of Tully Lake is agate brown because of the bogs which feed it with their overflow. Bog water is acid; and it is this that accounts for the small size of the numerous trout.

The path comes into the open after I have struggled for ten minutes through the dense shrubs. It comes into the open if you call a miniature forest of bracken open ground. I wade through the bracken, and emerge on the stony tip of the island where the grass is tufted, showing that otters pass this way. Now, though the view of Half-Moon Island is unobstructed, not a heron is to be seen. They are away standing in the flags of some marsh or by the side of some tiny stream. Tully Lake is too deep for them to fish; and there is nowhere to stand in its reeds. One of them has gone to a station of his own by Roisinduff Lake two miles away. Roisinduff means 'the Little Dark Wood', and the lake is called after it. Some of that ancient wood still remains to justify the name that the old Irish, who were susceptible to the features of the landscape that surrounded them, gave to the Lake of the Little Dark Wood.

I know that heron's post well. It is where the water-lilies are huddled at the western side of the lake. One bird rose when I was going round the lake some days ago and flew away over the rising ground on solemn wings. He did not fly home to Tully Lake, for I watched him that was watching me; but he went out of sight where the land falls to the beach. There is a trickle of water there where a frog may swim.

If I lie down I might as well close my eyes because—I may as well acknowledge it—I cannot stand the sight of beauty for more than ten minutes, if so long. The view of the Benna Beola—the Twelve Bens—with the gold dust in the air that fills their valleys, because for me it is inexpressible, fills me with unrest. It is the same when I gaze upon a sunset over the Atlantic by Roisinduff. The sun sets behind the island of Inisturk and turns its purple into black with a luminosity in it. It would be hopeless to attempt to describe this—just as hopeless as it is to turn the Twelve Bens into words, because it is not the description but the spirit of the sunset that should glow in a single happy word. It would hurt too much to search it out. It would mean walk after walk through the wild wood; so be content to stare a while at the mountains, then close your eyes and hope that the everlasting mountains will take their place.

Why the devil I should want to stuff a sunset into one word I do not know. In the first place, no word could contain it; in the second place, there is no one word for it; and in the third place, if there were, I would not be competent to find it. So I may as well feel beauty while I last and cease to torture myself by trying to express it.

The aborigines who lived on the third island in this lake must have felt the beauty of their surroundings deeper far than I, for it was innate. When the last late Government tried to set their descendants down in the fallow lands of Meath, these mountainy men developed a homesickness that amounted to a disease.

Yes; south of Half-Moon Island is a round island not much larger than a tennis-court. It was once surrounded by large stones which were removed when old Blake, the Sunday man, built a cottage on Freilaun. A Sunday man is not necessarily a devotee, but one who could move freely only on Sundays, for on that day the King's Writ did not run; and debtors were safe. Blake removed the encircling stones and with them traces of one of the oldest of habitations—a dwelling on a crannoge or island (usually artificial) in lake or marsh. These may be compared to the pile-dwellings in the lakes of Switzerland. Why men wished to crowd on an island little larger than a large room is hard to say. It may have been to keep their children safe from the wolves that were a pest that could not be exterminated. Whatever compelled them who can tell? But that they lived on the crannoge in Tully Lake is indisputable: their bone needles were found there, and what else who knows?

So I am not the only one who saw the sun on the Twelve Bens and could only point to it. If you want to feel more than sensation can take, come and see it for yourself.

Why should I linger beyond the scent of the woodbine? I will go back to the shelter of the lawn. There, beside a bush of broom and under a bank of wild roses, I will gaze at the screened water and cut off Eternity at both ends with the garden shears. Only by a garden shears may this be done.

There is light enough in June to go to bed without a candle; but a candle should be lit to bring back a forgotten light that is softer than electric light under the mellowest of shades. Bernard Shaw may have reason in keeping electric light out of his cottage. His reason cannot be that candle-light is more beautiful: he is thinking probably that the unknown rays of electricity are bad for his health; whereas candle-light is comforting. It is more soothing than electric light and easier on the eyes. It is astonishing how much light a candle can give. It is not enough for modern eyes to read by, though the greatest works in the world were written by it; but it fills a bedroom with a soporific glow.

It is important to quench a candle properly. If you do not, the smell of burnt candle-grease can keep you awake too long. It is bad enough to have the cuckoo's incessant song breaking the silence and bringing thoughts of the murder of birds of a better song, without a nasty smell in the room. Maybe, if I listen well, I can hear the water lapping; but all I can hear now is the occasional barking of a distant dog.

This is better than looking at a brick house on the other side of the street, I said when at breakfast I gazed through the window and saw walls of rhododendron mixed with mauve. The morning light was coming through the trees which veiled the upshot glitter from the water. All was very still. An ousel cock took courage and picked up the bread I threw upon the grass. But he must have seen me move in the room, for soon he took alarm and flew up into a tree.

I wandered down the path that leads to the little pier. What a sight was there! Two swans, stately on the water for all their wildness, moved slowly, dipping their necks for the red weed. This, it seems, grows only near the pier; and that is what brought the two swans so close to the shore. Between them six little grey cygnets, looking like floating balls covered with aigrette feathers, tried to imitate the parent birds, but their necks were far too short. The big birds kept the little ones between them to shelter them from the ripples and the breeze. I went back to the house for some bread; but the moment I raised my arm to throw it, they moved slowly but deliberately away. Leave them wild as they are. Why should lovely things be made dependable on crumbs from a man's table?

This is the first time that swans have hatched out on Tully Lake. On the upper lake there have been two swans for twenty years. They hatch out their eggs every two years, and drive their offspring away as soon as the white feathers take the place of the light brown. They are sent to fend for themselves by being driven out to sea, for Roisinduff is separated from the sea by only a ridge of beach fifty yards wide. Maybe the two on Tully Lake were swans cast out of Roisinduff. It is pleasant to think of these beautiful wild things neighbouring me so near. I am glad that there are no pike in the lake to drag their little ones down. There are no pike west of Lough Corrib, for Lough Corrib is a Rome to them from which no one runs away. They grow to such a size in that lake that they could attack and kill a swan. That must be why there are no wild swans on Lough

Corrib. It makes my two wild swans all the dearer to me.

I have found a perfect way to observe the sportsman's ritual, which is to fish wherever there are trout. No lake in Connemara has more trout than Tully Lake or trout that are easier to catch. So, to prevent endless questions, 'What luck to-day?' 'What fly did you put up?' 'What's your heaviest fish?' I take the boat by myself and fish with neither fly nor hook upon the cast. After a little, good-natured people do not like to ask questions that would show me up as a far-from-Compleat Angler. I know that they pity me in their piscatorial hearts. I pity the fish. So the two pities balance one another. Meanwhile I can take a boat and drift on the lake without rumours getting about regarding my eccentricity.

This is not an original idea. I got it from the Chinese poet, Ching Chi Ho. He was banished from Court, so he spent his time in fishing; but, determined not to be disturbed, he used no bait. He probably did not use a hook, for you never can be sure that a fish may not take a hook just as well as a fly. At last, he was recalled from exile; but he refused to leave his fishing and his peace. I remember being so struck by the wisdom of the man that I tried to celebrate him in verse. I never can remember my own verses. To this I owe the remnant of my friends; but, if I can put my hand on the book,

I will, by your leave, reprint the verses I made in honour of the fisherman to whom I owe my peace.

Another reason makes me loath to fish: I have a pet fish, an angel fish, round as a silver coin, and ruffled with two little fins swift as the wings of a bee. He has two long whiskers like a Chinaman's, which droop down from each side of his mouth as he swims to the side of his aquarium to look out for me. I feel that I could hardly face him again if I were the slayer of dozens of his kin who are all too easy to catch. So don't shout at me, 'Hi! You have forgotten your landing net!'

ANGLERS

That pleasant Chinese poet, Chin Chi Ho,
Who spent his time in fishing with no bait,
Recalled at last from exile, would not go
And leave the stream where he could meditate
And foil all interrupters with his ruse,
Sitting beside the water with his line.
Was it a wonder that he should refuse
When he could catch his rhythms half asleep,
Watching below the lilies fishes shine
Or move not—it was all the same to him—
And river mosses when he gazed more deep,
And deeper, clouds across the azure swim?

There's not a roof now on the courts whose schemes
Kept men awake and anxious all night long
Distracted by their working out; but dreams
He dreamt in idleness and turned to song

Can still delight his people. As for me,
I, who must daily at enactments look
To make men happy by legality,
Envy the poet of the baitless hook.

For the last week I have not seen the swans and their cygnets. They may be sheltering behind one of the islands, for the Summers here are not as assured as those of Maine or Vermont—Vermont, the county of America that most resembles Ireland. Even with the shelter of Letter Hill the wind from the Atlantic cannot be kept out. It does not whistle round the house, for that is embowered; but it blows white crests on the lake. If there is red weed only by the pier, it must go hard with the swans to find food in Tully Lake. Their young cannot be more than three weeks old. They are too young to fly, so they must be here.

The bell on the farther pier is ringing. That is the way the postman shows that he has come with the mail. He is an impatient fellow. The extra half-mile to the lake is an unwelcome stretching of his daily round. He waits for only two minutes. If no boat puts out within that time you have to wait until next day for your letters and newspapers. Not that I miss newspapers, for I make my own news here. But now I take the oars and put my back into it as I row to the shore.

I had to go to the hotel beside the upper lake. I

met the chauffeur on my way, and he gave me a lift. He was coming for me in any case. He had a tale to tell that had him all mixed up. He was incoherent.

'It's a tragedy and no mistake!'

But to question him only made him worse. He hung his head.

'The swans?' I asked, fearing the worst. He nodded.

'A tragedy and . . .?'

At first I got it all wrong; but after a while I had it all straightened out. The parent swans had taken their young ones to Roisinduff Lake, and were driven off by the old couple who had held that lake for twenty years.

'And every time the male bird drove the other off, he killed a young one.'

'And you did nothing?'

'I went for my gun to shoot him, but by the time I got back it was too late.'

It was a tragedy 'and no mistake'. It saddened and silenced me. I knew now why I had missed my little birds. Then, realising that they could not fly, I asked the chauffeur how they got to the upper lake.

'There's a story in that. They walked them all the way.'

I asked, 'Do you mean to tell me that the swans trekked the two miles by road? Why, the cygnets were too small to reach it through the bog. They would have been lost.'

'It took all day from three o'clock in the afternoon until sunset. The Civic Guard held up a truck that was going up the lane while they were moving; and you should have seen the old birds keeping the small boys away.'

Two miles by crooked lanes and road! The parent birds must have observed the way they would have to go from the air, and they had learned the route well, because from the ground they could see nothing but the hedges and the stone walls that hemmed them in.

'Did they go across country at all?'

'No. They went all the way by boreen and road until they came to the lake. And then the fight took place. I was on the other side of the lake, so I could do nothing until it was all over.'

For days I was depressed. I cannot look at the pair of swans on the upper lake as they float about, keeping a few yards apart, or shine by the side of the little flat green islet where they nest. That is what caused the fight. The older couple were nesting. I found that out when I questioned the man again. He told me that they had three eggs, one of which was light. He threw that one away. After what must have been more than the usual five or six weeks, when nothing appeared, he threw the other two away.

I did not thank him for his interference or for his lack of it. I pondered on the design of Nature that two swans that may have been too old to produce living progeny should have killed six healthy little ones.

Why, I have often asked myself since, did the parents who were clever enough to follow paths mapped from the air, hatch out their six eggs by a lake that was deficient in food to feed them. Obviously, it was the dearth of food that made them take to the land and lead their young to a lake that, because of its muddy bottom, is rich in all kinds of water-plants. Roisinduff is rich indeed. In it a water-fern has been found the like of which has been found in only one other lake, and that is in Cumberland.

'A tragedy, and no mistake!'

There has been so sign of the bereaved couple since. I wonder where they are gone. They may have gone to Kinvarra, where there are a games of swans, fifty or sixty in number dipping for whatever the subterranean river from Coole which emerges beside the old castle of Dungory, brings down from the Seven Woods.

I hope that, wherever they are, they do not associate the murder of their little ones with a man who may have frightened them off when he tried to throw them bread.

CHAPTER FOURTEEN

The Many-Coloured Land

WHEN AN ISLAND becomes too small it is time for a ramble on the mainland.

I often dream of a pool of water crystal clear; now, with water all about me, I think of a pleasant lane that leads to wherever I will.

It is no farther than the swans went on that fateful journey; but I must not burden my memory 'with a heaviness that is gone'.

There is a grass border all along the boreen: wider on the left just as you enter it. Here tinkers come camping once a year. There must be a well somewhere in the reeds; but that is off the path, and I am not going to be diverted by water just now. The lane is hedged by dark-green furze without a yellow flower. This is strange. They say that 'Love is out of season when the gorse is out of bloom'. I do not wish to be an augur. Love is still able, even in Ireland, to take care of itself, blossom or no blossom on the gorse. I will leave it at that and walk along. One thing that delights me is that no gardener ever came here. Whatever grows planted itself; and did it well. There is just enough rough gorse to make the wild rose all the rarer and to keep the loops of the blackberries down. I notice one wild rose mixed so well with woodbine that it seems to have a double flower and two scents. It was 'quite canopied o'er with luscious woodbine' as it leant across the path. One good thing about woodbine is that it never strangles the shrub or tree that sustains it, whereas ivy kills whatever it embraces. No; I will not bore you by drawing a moral from that! Like most morals, it is all too obvious and trite. This is a lane in which it is better to linger than to go on. I will hasten slowly on my way to the sea behind Letter Hill. There, on the edge of the Atlantic, amid the many coloured mountains on the outermost shelf of Europe, dwell men who speak the immemorial tongue that sweetened the air long before the English language came out of the German lowlands. Centuries before Langland struggled with his stark monosyllables the Gael was speaking and singing in a flexible speech full of innumerable nuances of soft sounds. I am still in this winding lane with its ample grassy margins and inextricable tangle of wild flowers, bounded by walls seen here and there of mottled grey: a lane after my heart, unspoilt by man's regulations, free from all pruning, weeding or manuring, decent to last in its own order when all gardens are overgrown; a lane to go back and forth in; a lane I am loath to leave until somebody tells me that to *Lecanora parella* is due the mottling of the stones.

While I am enjoying this freedom from all formality, this garden in a waste, the thought is borne in on me with its questioning, 'What hope is there for anyone like me whose mind is fed on wildness, who resents all hints of the law behind order and is, nevertheless, elated and content?' This is more than the problem of the effect of environment on the creature, instead of what you might think should be the other way about. It is the problem of all Ireland except, perhaps, that constricted corner of Ulster where all is orderly and therefore ordinary. There the 'subjects' pay with all the Arts for their model farms; but I was born free. Cajoled by bigotry and distracted by a Saturnalia (in the middle of Summer!) in honour of a King who was a pervert, it never dawns on them that they are being exploited and enslaved. Their docility is dangerous. Like the slavery of Russia, it is a menace to the world. The graces of civilisation are withheld from them. For poetry they are given "resolutions"; for painting, Orange banners; and for music, fifes and drums. And in spite of all this they are not blind. Never forget that it was the Belfast University that was the first to honour Yeats, while the University of his natal town was dumb—the Silent Sister. There are no sex-starved censors in the North. And it was a Belfast bookseller who said, on reading *As I was Going Down Sackville Street*, 'If this isn't the best yet, may I die in a temperance hotel!'

Behind me rise the purple mountains diamonded by a flash of sunlight or merging into the majesty of purple and gold. Before me lies the illimitable Atlantic, whereon float spectral islands seen once in seven years. Thus, once upon a time floated the Isle of Inis Bofin—the Isle of the White Cow—until it was accidentally disenchanted by some fishermen who touched it with fire. It could no longer float hidden from mortal eyes, for fire had the power to fix it forever on its base. This is the way that came about. From Omey Island, which can be reached from the mainland at low tide, went a fisherman and his son with a seed of fire laid on clay to broil the fish they might catch. They were not many hours out at sea until they heard about them the song of birds and the sounds of sheep and lambs. They thought that they had reached Hy Brasil; so they landed, bringing with them their catch of fish and their fire. They looked about. They beheld a lady full beautiful driving a cow that was no mortal cow to a lake. She touched the cow, and it turned into a stone. One of the fishermen went to remonstrate with her, and she instantly became a rock.

Before any disaster the White Cow can be seen on the island which is inhabited by mortals now. This is a part of a legend, a part, much garbled, of mythology older than Ireland of the Moon Goddess in her three aspects. She is the lady 'full beautiful'; she is the White Cow and, lastly, she is the rock. But let us leave such exactness to mythographers.

Though the cow and its lovely herdess are petrified, nothing has happened to the fairies who can be heard carousing in the hills. They tempt men to eat their fairy food by throwing down showers of fish. A man who was going by the side of a rath or fairy fort was struck by an iris leaf thrown by one of its inhabitants; he drew his black-hafted knife and stabbed the elf. Terrified by what he had done, the fairy-killer ran for help and, on returning with some men, found only a heap of slime, 'like what a dead frog turns into', on the spot. An Englishman who lived there until recently declared, one day, he went out shooting, that he was surrounded by a troupe of fairy girls dressed in brown.

The long mountain at last falls into the sea with many a gully and indentation. Some of these were caves and roofed over within memory; but the ocean sent its sappers under them and blew their roofs off.

Cave na Mbhan is one of these. This is called in English the Cave of the Women; and legend has it that the bodies of two naked women were found floating there. As for the date, you will get no information, for exactness in dates is unknown; but if you refer it to ' the days of the Spanish Armada ' you will be met by no denial, for that date embraces a lot of the romantic past. The Spanish Armada should be nothing to make dates by, for the way the survivors were treated on the west coast of Ireland is one of the disgraces of history.

The Cave na Mbhan had an interest for me because between the two world wars a merman was seen in it by two fishermen who told me about it by the aid of a ' witness ' who had wished himself in on them.

Here in Connemara a ' witness ' is a specious fellow who helps out unsophisticated people up before a magistrate for any misdemeanour or who happen to be the heroes of any event. He is the self-appointed counsel who, during the lunch hour, can weld the evidence and strengthen his clients' oaths. At other times such as this he is a ' producer '.

The story of the merman who haunts the coast of Connemara is too well known to be retold. It got full publicity in the English Press. Scientists explained him. 'It is possible that he may be a straggling dugong,' Dr. Lepper, a member of the Royal Zoological Society, said. 'This very warm weather might bring a straggler; but it is a long way from the Amazon to the west coast of Ireland. The description given by the fishermen seems to me impossible. More probably the fishermen saw a great grey seal.'

Yes; it is a long way from the Amazon, but not from Hy Brazil. And I have yet to meet a Connemara fisherman who would not recognise a 'great grey seal'. They are all over the littoral waters. I shot half a dozen of them in less than half an hour not so many years ago. Regan and Hearne, men who have spent all their lives—except the years they were in the first world war—on the sea, are not unlikely to recognise a seal however 'great' when they see one. The great grey Atlantic seal is the enemy of all who go down to the sea to fish.

Now that the witness who came with them when they first told me of the merman is not about, I can renew acquaintance with them and talk about something else.

I passed the old castle that had had stone cannonballs stuck in its masonry. It is known as Renvyle Castle, and is said to have been cannonaded by that masculine sea-queen, Grace O'Malley, or in Gaelic, Granu Maille.

Round the western shoulder of Letter Hill I went until I came across one of the two men, the one who had a limp from a severe knee-wound he got in the war.

'It's a long time since we met,' he said.

I said that it was. There was a pause. I broke the

silence. 'I often wanted to ask you why is "Fir na Mara" not used in Gaelic for the murruman or Man of the Sea?'

He smiled tolerantly, as well he might, for he had heard the old language in his cradle; and he spoke it mellifluously.

'That's schoolmasters' Irish,' he said.

'Schoolmasters' Irish,' I repeated, and smiled, for now I realised with what feelings the real Irish speakers regard compulsory Irish. The stuff that is forced down the necks of their children in the schools.

He repeated 'merriman' for me. This is about the nearest I can get to the sound in English letters, the nearest I could get to it in any alphabet, for my ear is incapable of following the fine inflexions he put into the word.

'They will never teach Irish by compulsion. Nothing can be achieved by compulsion in this country,' I assured him. 'It's significant that there's more Gaelic in the Highlands of Scotland than there is here in its home.'

'And wouldn't you think that they ought to know?'

'What makes it more foolish,' I said, 'is that the principal enthusiasts are outsiders who never heard a word of Irish until they came into this country. Now they're all for it, although they cannot pronounce a syllable of it correctly. Under their tutelage it bids well to disappear as unpopular as any political shibboleth can be. They cannot speak a sentence that you would understand.'

'But a schoolmaster might,' he said with a smile, 'if they paid him well.'

'I read the other day that one of those fellows whose name is full of English letters staggered, lamented the fact that Gaelic is disappearing. Is it any wonder? The kind of stuff they're teaching now is not only killing Gaelic but making the girls disappear. The "language", instead of preserving the national spirit, is emptying the nation; over to England they go. When they come back,' the speaker said, 'they despise all things Irish. Pseudo-Irish, I would say. But do you know what's driving them out?'

'What would that be?'

'Boredom, boredom and more boredom. They are bored stiff by all this artificiality. If a Government bores people, it will empty the country of all its girls and boys. Either to Hell or to Connaught; but even Connaught is emptying now.'

He cast an eye over the water to the West.

'It's not to America they're going, but to England,' I said, for I thought that, looking West, his mind was on the United States.

After a pause he sat on the wall on which he had been leaning when I spoke to him. I knew that he did not disagree with me; but, like all natives, he took not the slightest interest in the politics of the day.

'You have been about the world a bit,' I said. 'Do you know how Brazil came by its name?'

He shook his head.

'It got its name from Hy Brazil, the island of the Blest to which St. Brendan voyaged so far out there over the ocean. He thought that he sighted it in the setting sun.' And I pointed out to sea. By the depth of his silence I felt that he was gathering speech. But I went on: 'The Voyage of Brendan should interest all Irishmen. He may have been the first to discover what is now the American continent. He describes a floating island of glass. Which was scoffed at because no one recognised an iceberg from the description of one who saw an iceberg for the first time. On it were strange beasts with enormous teeth and speckled bellies: walruses evidently. When he reached the mainland he found no traces of the monks who went there before him. This looks like a forerunner of what happened to Columbus when he searched in vain for the settlement he had established on his first voyage. But this was in the sixth century of our era. Neglect of our legends, which are primitive history, is to blame for our ignorance. Anyway, he called his island Hy Brazil, which is now Brazil.'

Pensively he said:

'There's a lot of strange sights after sunset on the sea. Sometimes all the sea lights up; and you see what might be islands far out where you know that there is nothing—at least by day.'

Words in Gaelic from his cottage interrupted him. He asked to be excused and went in. In a minute he appeared again.

'That was griddle cake. The wife would like you to come in.'

I demurred.

'It's no trouble at all,' he said.

So I went in with him. The table was being laid for three.

The cottage, in spite of the smallness of its windows, was bright enough inside. The door was open, and that helped to light the room. There were flowers in a pot on one of the sills. A tall dresser held the family crockery: blue and shining. The woman of the house dusted a chair for me and we sat down. There was yellow butter *go leor* and griddle cake. I had to ask for hot water to dilute the tea. If I drunk it as strong as it was, I would have had palpitation of the heart for the rest of the day. I felt that they pitied me.

Tea is the principal stimulant of the fisher folk; Indian, not China tea.

'Tim was telling me that he went to see you about the Merriman.'

'Yes,' I said casually. 'Years ago.' For I did not wish the woman to think that the sole object of my visit was to make more inquiries. It was a friendly visit, and to be treated as such. So I waived the Merriman off with, 'There's been too much talk about such things. Not that the newspapers believe them anyway.'

This had the effect of putting our hostess on her mettle.

'If they lived here they'd be wiser. But maybe they're better where they are.'

'Much better,' I heartily agreed.

'The butter's at your elbow. You're eating nothing.'

'I was thinking all the more,' I said.

Innate courtesy forbade her to enquire concerning the subject of my thoughts.

She stood up and filled my teacup. Then she passed me a jug of milk. That was a sign that her interest had not relaxed, so I went on:

'We were talking about St. Brendan when he sailed to Hy Brazil, having sighted it at sunset out to the West; and about the islands that appear as if they were enchanted.'

She remained silent when I ceased. After the pause she said, '"Enchanted" is right. And why wouldn't they be?'

I pleaded ignorance, hoping to be informed.

'The old people do be telling of a queer island. It's an old story that it was reached by fishermen years and years ago. Hy Brazil you were talking about. It was Hy Brazil they landed on, and there was people to report it, too. Thousands of people seen it from the North. But this captain—he was more than a fisherman—if I remember rightly, he was a sea captain who used to sail to France. One time he was sailing out from Donegal or wherever he was. He found himself in a thick fog, so thick that he couldn't see the sides of his ship from the middle. He couldn't tell where he was, so he took soundings and let the vessel drift. It got shallower and shallower, and at last it got so shallow that he knew he must be near land, so he let the anchor drop. When he looked up, what did he see but an island with horses, cattle, sheep and black rabbits. That ought to have been enough to scare him out of his life. He took no notice; but went ashore with eight of his company; and after walking for a while they came to a castle and knocked on the door. Nobody answered no matter how loud they knocked. They walked all round it; but they couldn't get in. So they gave up and started to light a fire to cook a bite to eat. All of a sudden they heard a terrible noise. They took to their heels and made for their boat and rowed out to the ship. In the morning they saw a gentleman and his attendants on the shore and he waving to them. After a while they made up their minds to send the boat for him, and they brought him off. It was a queer story he had to tell them, I wouldn't go so far as to say that I believe it or not.'

She paused, and asked if we wanted more tea.

'That'll do you now. Go on with your story,' her husband said. He probably resented an artist's subterfuge to add suspense and relish to the tale.

'He said that he and his servants had been imprisoned in the castle by an enchanter; but that lighting a Christian fire wrecked the tower and broke the spell.'

'Only for that it might be fair enough,' her husband acknowledged. To him the enchanted island was apparently acceptable.

'I'm only telling you what I heard myself. I'm not making it up like a shanachie as I go along.'

'We know that. We didn't mean to interrupt you.'

But, like the castle, the spell was broken.

'Well, that's all there is to it,' she said, and began to clear the table.

'Regions which are fairyland,' I said to myself, but I could not help thinking that we might have heard more but for the man's taking exception to the enchanted castle. An enchanted island, yes; he had seen them off and on, but he had not landed on any of them.

Many of such tales have root in fact. Time, and that sibness to the supernatural which is the heritage of the Gael, exaggerate and magnify them until the historian loses patience. But when I remember the accounts of how savagely the Armada crews were treated by the Irish natives who despoiled them, stripped and clubbed them to death, having robbed them of their silks and jewels, I thought the story highly plausible. Suppose some island chieftain had imprisoned some suppliant grandee who, with the surviving members of a broken ship, had sought sanctuary with him who presumably was no friend of England and not afraid to defy her orders to kill all sailors of the Armada who tried to land, and who was holding him to ransom while awaiting the news from Spain; and that during the period of his incarceration some men landed on his island who looked like guardians of the coast, would he not have released the Spaniard for fear lest he should get into trouble with the authorities? If you substitute one kind of fire for another and read 'cannon' instead of 'Christian fire', the account of the cracked tower is not incredible. Grace O'Malley herself might have been the enchantress of the tale. It's a thing that you couldn't put past her, anyway.

By low stone walls white with lichen like flakes of flat foam, I walked back to the island, encouraged by the story I had heard for the evidence it gave of insistence on the supernatural. Nothing less will satisfy the Gael.

In this day of ours, when the seat of the spiritual impulses of man is placed in the lower bowel by a quack like Freud, one of the most prominent of the '*hostes humani generis*' of our time, it is refreshing to listen to a tale of something beyond the reach of psychoanalytic frauds. It saddens me to think of the seriousness with which such pseudo-scientists are accepted by an all-too-gullible public. I had leifer live in Belfast, that bright suburb of Glasgow where there are psychic cases only on one day in the year, than among those who believe in the constraining influence of the bowel on the soul. And no one sees the cynicism.

Compared with the treatises you read on anal fixations and other indecencies, the story of the enchanted islands of the West is sweet as morning dew and as fragrant as a lane lined with honeysuckle.

Were it not for the clouds off the Atlantic that break in rain, I would never leave Renvyle with its glimmering islands and its assured faith in wonders of the deep.

CHAPTER FIFTEEN

The Spirit of the Place

BY THIS TIME it should be pretty obvious who is the hero of this narrative. It is certainly not the writer. Who then? The country is the hero, the landscape if you like to call it that, or the *genius loci*, the spirit of the place, the pull of the earth, that nucleus smasher which can transmute anything. And, this being so, the history of the hero's vicissitudes is not out of place, even if we have to go back some time to find his lean years. I remember before an election—there were plenty of elections then if the Government found itself shaky—a gardener came to me to get my signature on his application for a blind pension.

'But you are not blind,' I objected, for I knew him well.

'I know that, sir; but I'll only have to go blind for a month or so, at the worst six weeks, till the election.'

'But why do you want to go blind?'

'Well, it's like this: them rabbits is a pest.

They're eatin' all the grass. If I get the pension, I can buy a gun.'

In a Democracy it is very hard to prevent the country's money from being spent to return the gang to power or to keep it in power. But this being Ireland, it is not always the vote that is cast for efficiency.

There was a commercial traveller who visited a small village in which were two gombeen men—that is, two principal merchants who between them had the whole village on their books from which there was no escape, short of a windfall.

He solicited one of the merchants, 'I have not had an order from you for over a year.'

'And you'll get none. My business is ruined. The country's business is ruined, too. I'm burst. I'm bankrupt!'

'Well, you know who you voted for at the last election.'

'And I'll vote for him again; for that old blackguard up the street is not bankrupt yet.'

Those were the days when the bus drivers and conductors looked forward to an election to improve the roads. It seemed that there was some connection between the state of the roads and votes. So money was lavished upon the roads until they became literally paved with gold, like the fabled streets of New York.

A vibration which caused me to bite my tongue shook the bus. The conductor was all sympathy.

'If it were not so full I could put you in the middle seat. There you'd find it easier.'

We were speeding along the road that Morton, who goes 'in search' of countries, declared to be the loveliest in the world, the road to Clifden; but we were travelling in a direction the reverse of his, for Clifden we had just left.

Ballinahinch would soon be reached, with its glimpses of the salmon-pools into which the Indian Maharajah, Ranji Singh, had piers built wherever a salmon had risen. Now, if it had been the Ganges, it might have been a considerable gesture in honour of the crocodiles; but a Connemara salmon could only regard the unusual obstacles as a few more boulders fallen from the hills, and changed his accustomed ways. It was hard to understand and impossible to explain. It would be worth while to have a few words with the gillie.

The bus was bounding along beside the ruined bridges and the grass-grown permanent way of the old Galway–Clifden train which it had superseded. Bounding, bounding along mile after mile *et nos mutamur in illos*. However, it was not my stomach that changed; but the stomachs of two children to whom the motion was a novelty. Send us an election soon, O Lord!

We passed a lake with one island on which there was a solitary pine. I remembered how once, early, before the morning mist had risen, that pine appeared out of a wall of luminous grey as if it were the work of some artist of China, one of those who knew how to paint mists so well. It appeared to be in the middle air, for the lake was as yet invisible, and so the level of the pine could not be judged. The lake itself was hidden, but the stream that ran into it was coloured like claret in the level light. The Many-coloured Land!

The country opened as the Twelve Bens receded. The wet, yellow-green fields spread fenceless, for 'drains' took the place of fences or stone walls. A bridge with three arches of dark stone told of a road over a stream. Somewhere to the left a farm would soon come into view, a farm that was a most attractive arrangement of stone walls terraced in irregular lines on the side of a hill. A well-kept stone cottage unwhitewashed with lichened walls above and beside it made a symphony in grey. It was as if the stony heart of the land had been conjured and compelled to turn into a house with garden and garth walls all of living stone.

Soon came Ross House, or rather the grounds of what had been Ross House, for on the left we passed torn trees and broken walls, a broken gate that closed the entrance to what was once the avenue had been knocked down.

A cottage with garden walls had been built with stones from the fields, some of which had been carved with all the taste of the XVIIIth century. A prosperous tavern stood on the sweep which fronted the gate in the days gone by. Here the Earl of Mayo's remark would be out of place. The Land Commission are landlords now, and have but little feeling for 'demesnes'. The long-dead owner, Martin of Ross, wrote a comic Irish song. Probably, like Percy French, he soothed his broken heart with comic songs. It will be some time before a song sounds in Ireland again: anyway, not until after the election. When it does it may not be whimsical. Even our humbugs are melancholy now. Why? Some people cannot take affluence. It saddens them. Maybe, they pretend to be sorrowful like Tim Healy when he became Governor General lest people might think that he was too well off.

Somewhere between Moycullen and the town of Galway two lofty piers rose gateless. There is no sign of them now.

'Could those be the gate-posts of the long avenue of Ballinahinch Castle?' I asked and, as I feared, the question implied a history too old for a man of the conductor's age.

The story went that Martin of Ballinahinch—'Humanity Dick' as they called him for his Prevention of Cruelty to Animals Bill—was walking with George IV in Windsor Great Park (a little holding of seven hundred acres) when the King asked if he had anything as extensive in Ireland.

Martin replied:

'My avenue is fifty miles long.'

He might have added that his property in which His Majesty's Writ did not run was well over a hundred thousand acres.

We had travelled about fifty miles from Ballinahinch. Very likely the pillars we passed were the entrance gates to Martin's avenue.

Menlo Castle stood black and bare over the Corrib to the left. Menlo, a name carried by the Olivers of Galway as far west as San Francisco, is another ruin not caused this time by the civil war, but by a demented sister of Sir Valentine Blake who, wandering with a lamp one night, set the oak panelling on fire; and the ancient pile went up like matchwood.

Sir Valentine Blake was a famous character. He drank a British Admiral off a gang-plank. That is, the Admiral, who had pitted himself against the strong-headed knight, fell off his gang-plank as he was returning to his ship. A story made apocryphal, however, by the fact that Galway Harbour could not accommodate a battleship and there are no gang-planks between a launch and a vessel's side.

Nevertheless, Sir Valentine was a good man at bingling. He was of so hospitable a frame of mind that Lady Blake kept the keys of the tantalus, so Sir Valentine had to plead the laws of hospitality when he saw the District Inspector of Police driving briskly to the castle with his small son beside him. Sir Valentine demanded the key. It would never be said that Menlo could not offer a guest refreshment. There would be two.

Later, he set the minds of his visitors at rest, for the fire in the haystack which he had come to investigate was not a case of malicious damage, but had been set by Sir Valentine so that he might have the pleasure of the Inspector's company.

A man of great originality was Sir Valentine, who could use fire to quench a thirst!

The conductor's shout, 'You've made it!' aroused me from my reverie. He meant that the bus had arrived in time for me to catch the train to Dublin.

I looked in vain for a railway porter. Apparently the feud between the services was not over. No railway porter would deign to handle luggage degraded by a bus. A cheerful, toothless little fellow who answers to the Chaldean name of 'Seorsam' came from nowhere and refused to unload any luggage but mine. Some minutes elapsed before I could point out to him my baggage on the top of the bus. I feared that the engine-driver might share the porter's resentment and drive off without me.

' He belted her along well. You're in plenty of time. The guard has not come along yet.'

' Nevertheless,' I said, ' put those bags in a carriage for me."

" I'll leave them where you can't miss them."

He took them away and laid them by one of the doors that gave on the platform. Further entry evidently was denied him. I took the lightest bag and placed it in a carriage. I hoped to reserve a seat by doing so. I directed a listless youth who was the solitary porter to add the rest. I went back to look for my uniformed assistance. He found me. He ignored the late occupants of the bus. Evidently I had found favour.

' It's brightening up a bit,' he remarked. ' We've had a sprinkle and no mistake.'

' Will it keep off? ' I asked.

' They say in Galway that if you can see the Aran Islands, it's going to rain. If you can't see them, it's raining anyway.'

In the comfort of a railway carriage I put together the lines I had composed on the coming fate of the Dublin–Galway train. If you can take the ballad, here it is in the making, for once it is completed I shall cease to remember it. I leave it to you to say, ' That's just as well.' Don't forget that it was made in the lean year when you didn't know where you were going in Ireland.

CHAPTER SIXTEEN

ΠΑΝΤΑ ΡΕΙ

Everything changes:
Time deranges
Men and women and mountain ranges

Why the Devil can't Time let Wellenough alone?
He no longer stoops to set his '*Nil obstat*' on
Trusted, tried and comely things than he sekes to change,
Wither, age and alter them and the best derange.
This has happened just of late to the Galway train
That with passengers and freight crossed the central plain,
Pulling out from Dublin town that Liffey's stream divides
West to old grey Galway town, where Corrib meets the tides.
It strains at first, then settles down and smoothly rolls along
Past villages with Gaelic names that sweeten on the tongue:
Clonsilla, Lucan and Maynooth beside the long canal,
Where yellow-centred lilies float and no one comes at all,
The long canal that idle lies from Dublin to Athlone,
To Luan's Ford: but no one knows who may have been Luan,
The Royal Canal that joins two towns and makes of him a dunce
Who holds that nothing can be found in two places at once;
A long clear lane of water clean by flags and rushes rimmed,
Where, crimson-striped, the roaches steer, and, by the lilies dimmed,
The greenish pikes suspended lurk with fins that hardly stir
Until the Galway train comes on and shakes each ambusher.
The lovely hills are left behind; but soon the rising sun
Will overtop the mountain range and make the shadows run.

Παντὰ ῥει

The light that flushes the hills was low;
But now it gathers to overflow
And shadow each bush on the central plain
And gather the dews and catch the train.
And light the steam
In its morning beam,
Making a fugitive rainbow gleam.
Past walled Maynooth,
Where they teach the Truth
In the meadow called after Druidical Nooth.
Puff, puff!
That's the stuff
As if there weren't white clouds enough!

Like a charging knight with his plumes astream
The train comes on with its sunlit steam,
Past fields where cows are chewing the cud
To Mullingar, where the Square Mill stood,
Where the cattle-dealers, with rough red skins
And gaiters buttoned across their shins,
Wait for another train; they wait
For cattle-drovers to load the freight
Of blunt-nosed cattle with towsled coats
Bound for the East and the English boats:
Cattle-dealers replete with knowledge
That is not taught in an English college.

It blows
And goes,
A whale that feels
The pistons stabbing its driving wheels.

It reaches Moate, where a king lies still
Under the weight of a man-made hill.
On and on, until, quite soon,
It will come to the ford that was held by Luan,
Where, as in Spenser's pageantry,
The Shannon, ' spreading like a sea ',

Flows brightly on like a chain of lakes
Or linkèd shields that the morning takes:
The lordly stream that protected well
When jar-nosed Cromwell sent 'to hell'
The Irish nobles who stood to fight
That Bible-bellowing hypocrite.

From the bridge you can see the white boats moored,
And the strong, round castle that holds the ford.
Over the bridge it slowly comes,
The bridge held up on its strong white drums,
To enter Connaught. And now, good-bye
To matters of fact and Reality.
Ballinasloe, where the hostings were,
Ballinasloe, of the great horse-fair
That gathers in horses from Galway and Clare,
Wherever the fields of limestone are:
Mayo and Boyle and Coolavin
Between the miles of rushes and whin
And mountains high in a purple haze,
Streams and lakes and countless bays
Of Connemara, where still live on
The seaside heirs of the Sons of Conn.
To Athenry, where the kings passed by
From whom was named the Ath-na-Righ.
It rests for a minute at Oranmore,
A square grey castle protects the shore.
The Great Shore, limit of Galway Bay;
And Galway is only six miles away!

The engine-driver can wipe the oil
From his forehead and hands,
For his well-done toil
Is over now; and the engine stands
Only a foot from the buffer-stop
(He eased her down till he pulled her up).
Oh, see the children jump about
As doors are opened and friends come out

With paper parcels. What endless joys
Are hidden within those parcels of toys!
The county ladies in English tweeds,
With leathern faces fox-hunting breeds,
And shoes that give them a look of men,
Have come to the station 'just to look in'.
But never an officer home on leave
Is seen; instead, they only perceive
The rakel, card-playing boys debouch
And pay up their losses with search and grouch.
Oh, what a wonderful Noah's ark!
Lady Phillipa of Merlin Park,
Holding her parasol half up the handle,
Is back from Daly's of Dunsandle.
Where gold-headed Daly delights the gazers
As he leads the field of his Galway Blazers.
The Stationmaster opens a door
And clears a passage for Morty Mor,
For Morty Mor is known to own
The principal works of Galway town.
He is not one of the county set
(Though he helps them out when they lose a bet);
His saw-mills hum and he sells cement,
Potash and lime to his heart's content.
The workers he sacks on Saturday night
Are back on Monday morn contrite;
In spite of his temper, deep at the core
The heart's all right in Morty Mor.
That little boy lost is found again;
He ran away to the end of the train,
For all he can taste in his youthful hour
Of splendour and terror and speed and power:
The harnessed hates of water and flame,
The engine brings with its seething steam.

The platform now is empty again;
And empty stands the Galway train.

(Strange that nobody came to call
On the lonely men in the urinal.)
Land that is loved in ballad and song,
Land where the twilight lingers long,
May you be crossed and crossed again,
Forgetting the bus and the aeroplane,
By nothing worse than the Galway train,
Who shall tell how, when I'm dead and gone,
Gaily the Galway train came on?
How it puffed with pride on a road of its own;
How it whistled, *Waeshael!* to each nearing town;
How brightly its brass and its copper shone?
It seemed to be painted to match the scene
Of boglands brown and the trees between
With its coaches brown and its engine green.
It brought the towns where it stopped good luck,
Goods, the result of a bargain struck;
And it never ran over a cow or a duck.

Now all is changed for an overplus
Of passengers packed in a reasty bus,
A crowd that stinks and the air befouls,
And children pewk as the full bus rolls.
(A popular government plays to the masses
And that's what they get who abolish the classes.)
Lady Philippa, whose share of charity
Fails when it comes to familiarity,
Lady Philippa, her feelings hurt
Because Democracy means such dirt,
Is sitting, a most disdainful rider,
With the man from her gate-lodge sitting beside her.
The Law of Change would be just a jest
Were we sure that all change were a change for the best.

CHAPTER SEVENTEEN

Palmam Qui Meruit Ferat

I COULD SEE THE young poplars over the end wall of Ely Place as I was about to turn into it. I was not permitted to turn into it. One of those fellows whose names you never know, however well you may be familiar with the owner of the name, stopped me with a slow smile.

I was grateful to him for not asking, in that superior, half-aggrieved and wholly exasperating way, the question, 'You don't know my name?' Instead, he continued a conversation where he had left off ten years ago.

'As I was saying, that's a real anecdote, one that you could write.'

There are those who think that if something is recorded in writing, it becomes sacrosanct, immortal and no longer subject to the chances and changes of this mortal life.

'The story you told me?'

'Of course, what else?'

'Candidly, I have forgotten it. Let me have it again.'

In a swift, whispering voice he went on without pausing. The voice was not unpleasant. In fact, it was so soft and soothing that I was in danger of listening to the sound and not to what it conveyed, as the girls of Bryn Mawr listened to Æ. Swift as his utterance was, I could catch every word with little difficulty. I too was a citizen. The little Dublin man went on smoothly without inflexion.

'Surely you remember the story I told you about the Limerick Corporation and the aldermen who could not decide who was to be Mayor. If they voted among themselves, there would be a deadlock. That would never do. So, after much argument (I needn't tell you), they decided to repair to Thomond Bridge and to elect the first man who came across it. And who came across it but an upstanding young farmer leading a cart with creels of turf.

'"Would you like to be Mayor of Limerick?" they asked.

'"It would suit me nicely," says he.

'So they took him back and elected him Mayor; and Mayor he was, with the red velvet cushion in front of him and the mace on it. There's no telling the social reforms he made.

'One day while they were in session, his mother came to see him. There he was, Mayor of Limerick right enough. But he didn't seem to notice her. After looking at him awhile, she could stand it no longer.

'"Arrah, Pat!" she called out. "Don't you know yer own mother?"

'"I don't know meself," he said.

'You could make a good story out of that, particularly of the social reforms he put through.'

'What kind of social reforms?' I asked, suspicious as I am of all reforms.

'Wasn't he a farmer and didn't he know what the poor wanted. He was a socialist unbeknownst to himself.'

I thought for a moment. 'There's a story in that,' I acknowledge. 'And you have told it well.'

'Sure there is. And it's full of satire too.'

I turned as if to leave him, but he followed me to the end of Hume Street where it opens on Stephen's Green. Then he walked beside me. As if the thought impelled him, he took me by the arm.

'Do you know anything about palmistry? All the doctors are taking it up in Harley Street and lots of places.' Before I knew it, he had my right hand in his. He bent it back until the colour of the creases appeared. He bowed his head over it.

'Red!' he exclaimed. 'You're all right. Now, if those lines were yellow, it would mean anæmia. No; liver. If they were blue, it would mean that the auld ticker was out of order. I'm not coddin'. It's dead sure.'

He was so much in earnest that I could not bring myself to interrupt him.

'What a line of life you have! You'll live to be eighty.'

As much for his own information as for mine, he muttered in the same swift way, 'The Heart line; the Hill of Mars; the Line of the Head.'

I could not permit so much earnestness to go to waste. He 'intrigued' me, as the antique dealers say when they are pretending to be men of taste.

'You can't tell me what that line means,' I challenged, pointing to a transverse indented deeply into the ball of the thumb.

He was silent for half a minute by the watch; and that's longer than you would think.

'I'll tell you what that line means.'

'What does it mean?' I asked, for I had never heard it explained.

'It means energy. Anything on the ball of the thumb has to do with vitality. That line's for energy.'

I have had less pleasant readings by far. He left me thinking as much of myself as if he were a copy of the 'Reader's Digest' which aims at making you content. He had to go into his office, which was, oddly enough, you would think by the name of it, in the Board of Works. But not if you knew Dublin.

I went on my way rejoicing that I belonged to a city in which you can get a good story and have your hand read by a Civil Servant during the busiest hours under the chestnuts of Stephen's Green.

Ouspensky in one of his lectures in New York divided men into five classes or categories. The lowest two are more or less thoughtless automata who can speak only in clichés. The third are the 'self-conscious' class. Here 'self-conscious' is not used in the vulgar sense of shy or awkward, but in the sense of awareness of one's self as a rational being, one capable of reflection, of 'looking before and after'—in fact, individuals. The fourth class, geniuses, Plato, Shakespeare, Pasteur, Edison; the fifth, Avatars, Buddha, Confucius and the rest.

How does this apply to my subject which is of that city on the Liffey's banks and all that emerges therefrom or has to do with it? It explains why there are so many individuals in Dublin and why the first and second class—that of the robots—hardly is to be found in the old town. Everyone is of the self-conscious class, even if he rises only to a resigned self-pity, or, as is more frequently the case, to a self-righteous indignation against the slings and arrows, or against his fellow citizens.

Ouspensky would be as puzzled as Bernard Shaw if he came to Dublin.

There is something that has been puzzling me—worrying me, as they say in our town. It has no connection with Ouspensky's classifications, but it has to do with classifications of the literary figures in Ireland. The obstinate question is, Why is Dunsany not admitted into the hierarchy of the Irish Literary Renaissance? Before I could find an answer—an unsatisfactory answer at that—I had to determine who they were who decided who should be famous and who not. I found, alas, that the fame-makers were a little narrow and exclusive coterie the members of which excluded non-members from the pedestals they had assumed for themselves. This coterie consisted of the Directors of the Abbey Theatre which evaporated down to Lady Gregory. Her maternal and material instincts moved her to shoo off any possible rivals of herself and Yeats. Dunsany was the first to be ousted. There would be no pedestals for his Gods of the Mountain in the Abbey any more. Edward Martyn, one of the founders of not only the Literary Movement but of Sinn Fein, which was to free Ireland eventually, had been excluded from the very first. And yet he was one of Ireland's greatest sons, an aristocrat unashamed of his country.

In a less degree, for he never sought notoriety, Stephen Gwynn, one of the best poets Ireland has had for generations, soldier, sportsman, scholar, is hardly heard of in a Dublin that has run out of geniuses as the Abbey Theatre ran out of them when it sent out its S.O.S. in 1903.

Being as curious as an old Athenian, I asked one of the geniuses who remains why Stephen Gwynn was not acclaimed as he deserves. The answer was Delphic, 'He has written too many books.'

'But his poetry? His *Ossian and St. Patrick*; his poem of *Mary Queen of Scots* and, just lately and just as wonderfully as the eighty-year-old Robert Bridges, Poet Laureate's, *Testament of Beauty*, he has given us his *Salute to Valour*,' I asserted.

But it was the last oracle: Phoebus would speak no more. The water-springs were dead. But while she is being canonised, the *Advocatus diaboli* may submit that Lady Gregory was a fool not to welcome Dunsany. I, pleading for her beatification, will answer, 'No.' Dunsany was not unmonied. When it came to helping poets, he was not ungenerous, as, later, his support of Ledwidge was to prove. He might have been a greater patron of the Abbey Theatre than Miss Horniman. Why had he to go? For the same reason that Gregory of the Golden Mouth, as James Joyce irreverently called her, elbowed out Miss Horniman. Dunsany might prove troublesome. He might not be dominated. He might not kow-tow. He could not be closit in Coole.

And so the classifier, the fame-bestower, left him out. No chivalrous explanation, I admit; so, when a baron cannot wear a lady's favour, he espouses his own cause and tilts for himself.

This and other examples, Sean O'Casey to wit, may explain why the principal hero and heroine of the Irish Literary Renaissance are comprised in the Abbey Theatre coterie.

It must be admitted that Dunsany is difficult and indomitable—traits that were enough to disqualify him where compliance was indispensable. Dunsany is self-centred and a Conservative.

Then, too, there was not jealousy, but a certain hidden envy of the man. Yeats, who was feudal at heart, could not trace his ancestry back in Ireland to 1181, even though his family possessed a cup that had belonged to the Butlers of Ormonde: William *Butler* Yeats.

Stephen Gwynn is a scholar and a member of the great Trinity College family of scholars and sportsmen. If Trinity College was anathema, it was all the more unlikely that, in Dunsany's case, Eton and Sandhurst would be welcome. So Gwynn 'dwelt apart' as far as the Literary Coterie was concerned. The coterie is gone, but the impression remains that every gleam of Irish genius went with it. No critics, or reviewers or authorities can take genius to the grave with them.

Time holds a tribunal whose decrees are far more reaching than those of Lady Gregory. Before it, when Martyn, Dunsany and Gwynn come to be summoned, they will find themselves exonerated from contempt of the earlier court.

Lady Gregory would have excluded Tommy Moore for the reason that she excluded James Joyce: he was not quite a gentleman. Contrari-wise, I can imagine his indignation if, forty years hence, an historiographer were to discover Dunsany in the Fields of Dis with, " One of the Abbey Theatre, I presume? ' What a welcome he would get from the shade who had rhymed so lightly when on earth,

> ' I heard the pit and circle say,
> " Gregory bores us."
> As, one by one, they slip away.'

Disconcerting as it is to realise that everyone is fenced and bounded by the conventions of the time in which he lives, it is more irritating to know that by some accident you may be more accurately pigeon-holed in a particular compartment of time. Yeats and his contemporaries, for all their awareness of the narrowing effects of politics on poetry—an effect of which Thomas Davis was held to be the chief exemplar—owed their fame to being the mouthpiece of the popular myth of the time, and not, primarily, to their poetry. Yeats happened to be the greatest poet of the period because he had the gift of creating rhythm from the inner relation between words and metre. Had he to rely on this to recommend him to the populace, he would be as out of it as Dunsany is or as Milton was in Charles the Second's day.

What is the remedy? Obviously, the populace cannot be taught poetry in time to recognise it before an exponent dies. This would not be in the nature of things, seeing that every poet, if he is worthy of the name, must be prophetically ahead of his time and untrammelled as far as possible by its conventions. The remedy for the poet is not to seek public approbation but to flee from it as stigmatising him and dating him—*Odi profanum vulgus*. Let him look to his accomplishment for 'its own exceeding great reward'. This has been done before. If it bring no peace of mind it is because the poet has no confidence in his work. Flaubert cared little for applause. And I have yet to learn that Shakespeare signed anything but his will.

CHAPTER EIGHTEEN

Dunsany Castle

Follow the road along with me,
Mulhuddart first, and then Clonee,
Meath of the pleasant watercourses,
And Rogers rude who deals in horses.

I HAVE AN invitation to dine at Dunsany Castle whenever I can. I remember one invitation that was sent to me because it was in rhyme. I will quote only one stanza: the others are in Dunsany's *My Ireland*, one of the best books on that country.

'Here in this fertile land
The port you may not touch
Waits you, and by my hand
The wild duck slain and such.'

That was one of many hospitalities. But here it is due to myself to explain why I might not touch port, lest it be thought that I had achieved the last infirmity of idle limbs, gout. I had not even poor man's gout.

What had happened was that, influenced by the luxury and the feudal lordliness of his house, I had asked Dunsany where he bought his port.

'From Sir George Brooke.'

Now, the family of Dublin wine merchants known as Brooke were so well esteemed by those who could appreciate good wine (and consequently were in power) that they obtained a knighthood for the head of the firm. He became 'Sir George' just as Kay, in the court of King Arthur, was awarded the accolade.

To Brooke's in Gardiner Place I went and ordered some dozens of 'the kind of port you supply to Dunsany Castle'. Sir George himself had it looked up; and I got the wine in due course. The associations of the port turned me for a day or so into a two-bottle man. But oh, the difference to me!

All the cuckoo-clock factories of Switzerland moved into my skull. Every time my heel touched the ground four and twenty cuckoos began to sing.

I went rolling down the lea.

On my next visit to Dunsany I accosted my host. I told him what his dark brand of port had done, and of my martyrdom to his house. Such an imputation had never been heard before. He caused an inquiry to be made. The butler reported with becoming concern. It transpired that his predecessor had for years devoted himself to the castle's cellar, and after a life of assiduity, succeeded in drinking a pipe of port that had been laid down when His Lordship was born. The port with which the empty pipe was replenished was from one laid down on the birth of Dunsany's heir, who was in his cradle at the time. Dunsany's dark brand was also in its infancy.

Even though a general election was 'due any minute now' I could not wait for the work on the roads it promised. I went in a private car.

You do not enter Dunsany Castle by the great gate over which two white jennets support the baronial arms with the motto, *Festina lente*. The family name is Plunkett, which is a corruption of the Norman French for 'white jennet'. To enter by the great gate entails the opening of gates here and there in the park. So you go past it to Dunsany Cross, on the right-hand side of the road, and turn slant-wise through a narrow Gothic arch, hence a short drive which passes the old church on the left and one of the mottes, mounds or duns from which the place may have derived its name, brings you to the wide gravel sweep in front of the castle which rises sheer from the 'fertile land'.

The trees appeared to be thicker and heavier than they were ten years ago; but this must have been imagined by me, for few eyes can detect the growth of an old tree. Ivy there was in abundance. The old church to the left where the barons lie is clothed in the bright-green, shiny leaf. Little of the grey stone was visible. This was one sign of Time's passage. The walls of the castle, too, were green, not grey.

One tree stood shattered, but its cleft wood was almost hidden in foliage, for leaves in Meath are profuse.

The castle door is in the west tower, on the top of which Dunsany dreams and composes. He immures himself from noise, and any noise that reaches him from the broad meadows must be more muffled now, for the ivy vine has reached to the battlement. No one is permitted to see that skiey room which even the lowing of kine or the crowing of a cock can hardly enter. If no one may enter it but the poet, I felt that it was also forbidden to talk about it. I did not bring the subject up, for to do so might be construed as an attempt to get an invitation. He might not say it, but that is what he would think. But I wished ever so much to know if from its height—the Height of Constructive Contemplation, the Chinese would call it—the Boyne that became the Yann or the hills of Elfland to the south were visible as he looked over the desolate flatness that stretched to the rim of the sky and saw 'never a sign of Elfland, never a slope of the mountains', when the day threw off the blanketing clouds that comfort the herds of Meath.

Maunder, the stately butler who asked the Black and Tans as they were leaving the castle after raiding it, 'Who shall I say called?', did not come into the hall. Instead, an older man appeared, and said that his Lordship was in the billiard-room. I went straight back, for it is on the ground floor, and found him seated at a tea-table with light from the stained-glass windows throwing a nimbus around him and tricking my sight. He arose. In spite of his beard, he was no ' grey borderer on the March of death ', but incongruously sprightly. We discussed his work. I tried to get from him the origin of his wonderful names. Where did he get Narl and Zend and Lirazel; Pendondaris and Babbulkund? They flowed into his brain. They were not derived as Coleridge's Alph, the sacred river, was from Alpha, nor from the names of Indian villages where the tiger prowls. I should have guessed as much. For that which is breathed into us is ' inspiration ', and these names, each of which can translate the reader to translunary places, are certainly inspired.

A man grows older in proportion to the distance he passes beyond Keats. I find myself attracted by Matthew Arnold, the passionless school inspector, and by George Meredith, with Shakespeare as a standby before the end. Dunsany has translated Horace, the most complacent poet of them all.

We discussed Yeats's rudeness in turning his back on people. Dunsany derived it from Yeats's study of those who had turned their backs on him. Yeats, according to this theory, is presumed to have taken this as the ' normal gesture of a " gentleman " who wished to impress others with his superiority '; so therefore Yeats adopted it whenever he played the gentleman according to his interpretation of one.

I wondered where Yeats had met gentlemen with such conformity of conduct, for the few I have come across are more or less eccentric, and none of them has mannerisms in common. Besides, turning the back is more in keeping with a constable on point duty than with a gentleman. But that Yeats had an exalted and romantic view of those whom he elevated to the rank of 'gentlemen' cannot be denied.

My standards of sympathy and sentiment never alter. Yeats's memory and Dunsany's mind are equally inspiring to me. My only excuse for enjoying another's foibles is that I am not sufficiently aware of my own. Conscious of this, and not wishing to be discouraged, I never pray to any power for the giftie to see myself as others see me.

We were talking about the refusal of a knighthood by Yeats when Lady Dunsany came into the room. She pointed out that Kipling had done the same thing. This was an act on a par with Yeats's and just as inexplicable. She quoted from Kipling's *True Thomas*:

'And ye would make a knight of me!'

Obviously Kipling was disgruntled. He spent his leisure in making himself disliked equally when he lived in Vermont and Sussex. His ambition may have been a peerage such as Alfred Lord Tennyson achieved, or an Order of Merit. His case I could understand; but not the case of Yeats. Influences I could name (and did name) were at work to remind him that a *volte face* from a member of the Irish Republican Brotherhood to a Knight of the British Empire would be worse than Rolleston's coat-turning from an Irish Republican Brother to a censor of the books for Republican Brothers imprisoned in an English gaol.

All three are with the unaccoladed dead.

As I passed through the hall on my way out, I remembered more of my host's achievements.

The hall is half filled, if not adorned, by the head of a rhinoceros which thrusts its black snout three feet across the way. The white walls show up well the armour which covers them. There is a mace which was used for the laying on of hands by one of the Dunsany ancestors who was a bishop. He preferred a mace to a spear or sword, for the Church was averse to the shedding of blood; and he was a scrupulous Churchman.

Off the hall, and past the Magistrate's Room, is another deep in the tower. This room is decorated by the originals of Sidney H. Sime's drawings to illustrate Dunsany's earlier books, by some grotesque masks marvellously imaginative, made by the author, and a snake-skin the long tenant of which succumbed probably to a rifle-shot, for Dunsany is one of the best shots living. He shot a swallow in the wing with a rifle; but his modesty in sporting feats makes him attribute the fall of the swallow as much to the rifle blast as to good marksmanship.

The grotesque masks show another side of the artist which is concealed in his writings. They were the faces of denizens from some hollow or reversed Elfland. Yet there was no damnation or abomination of desolation about them, as there is in the great gulf where cackling laughter sounds in Joyce's last work. In some glass-topped case were engraved seals cut in silver.

Beside the fire a hidden door gives on what is now called a secret passage, but is in reality the winding stairs in the wall of the old tower, stairs such as all castles of the period have. This, then, is the way Dunsany climbed to the bedrooms of the visiting cricketers he haunted in lieu of a castle ghost.

I once suggested to the wise Mahaffy that the name Dunsany in its original form may have been 'Dunskeney', from the river Skene, which flows through the grounds, only to be met with the mild rebuke.

'My dear fellow, you will soon find out that in derivations the most plausible explanations are usually the least correct.'

I was not thinking about the Skene as a derivation of Dunsany now; but of it as the scene of an accident to his Lordship years ago when he had miscalculated the additional force the partial subsidence of the raft on which he was balanced would lend to the gunpowder in the torpedo with which he was experimenting when torpedoing himself. Gunpowder was in the blood. His father had a cannon charged with some sort of delayed or dud 'crack', so delayed that it blew the arm off the butler who was ordered to investigate it. It may have been an act on the part of Providence to get even with that unjust steward for his behaviour with regard to the pipe of port. I forgot to enquire if the butler died from the explosion or from his attempt to rival Perkaio, the dwarf who pitted his life against the contents of the great Tun of Nuremberg.

It is an open question whether or no Providence is concerned with port.

CHAPTER NINETEEN

Horse Race

'SPLINTER ME NECK!' said McGlornan. 'It's a damn fine Government. It represents the people better than the old gang. And it's not because anything would be better than what we've just had. It's the men in it. Decent men and an honour to the country. Only for the war we'd have got rid of the old gang years ago. What do you fancy for the first?'

We were at the races. McGlornan, restored to affluence and to some extent power as a backer of the new Government, was more interested in horses. This was as it should be. It was the first race-meeting since the general elections that had changed the face of things.

I am not much of an astronomer; but the sun seemed to have added a few more billions to its candle-power: the gloom that had depressed the day was lifted now. Even the weather was better.

'Hi!'

A well-known 'bookie' was opening the rumble

seat of his large sedan. In it was a bar fully equipped with liquid refreshments which could be used long before fatigue set in.

'I'll have to be going soon, but James will take care of you. See to them, James.'

It was not yet half-past twelve. As a rule I do not go to horse races; but if I have to go, it were well to go while there was yet a chance of getting a good place to park a car. But, early as it was, the enclosure was crowded without by the careless, happy-go-lucky tinkers, pedlars and fortune-tellers who come into being only at stated intervals which coincide with the different meetings which are held all over the island. You had to drive slowly while you ran the gauntlet of compliments (if there were women-folk with you) or abuse if you were travelling with male friends. Having shaken off a hundred offers of miscellaneous wares and dispensed a minimum of largesse, it was possible to drive the car across the rest of the field that circled the enclosure.

Do not become impatient with this noisy rabble. Theirs is a tradition older than history, a tradition that is contemporary with the first Fair or any assembly where men are gathered for sport. Bear, then, with the mockery, the cries, the ructions which will come later, and the cheers when any recognised personage arrives. They were at the Games of Taillteann, and they will be in Ireland as long as there is a horse left to run. They are the congregation of the Cult of the Horse.

That cult, in contradistinction to the Cult of the Cave, is observed in the open air, and its votaries are orgiastic and unrestrained. They are given neither to sorrow nor repentance. They feel dimly injured when subjected to the law.

These people, who would be called 'vagabonds' by the uninitiated, interested me more than the horses in whose honour the assembly was called. True it is, you could not have a race-meeting without horses. But neither would it be a meeting without the rabble without and the race-goers within.

'You must be having an anxious time now that Blethers is dead,' I shouted after the hospitable bookmaker.

Ted Blethers was a trainer who originally had come from England and, with an Englishman's sense of business, had become the leading trainer in the Curragh, which is the Irish Newmarket. He dominated the 'field'. Now that he was dead, the law of probability reigned again, and with it a certain amount of uncertainty which was enough to make any bookmaker anxious.

New faces were everywhere within the enclosure: pink Englishmen and brown foreigners; fat women who were not homebred, and the usual lanky hunting-women whom we all knew, and the hurried, busy, long-nosed men. For years I puzzled over the problem, how comes it that race-goers have long, pointed noses? You never see a snub-nosed jockey; but that is not a solution of the greater question. It is, of course, a well-known fact that devotees of any kind become to resemble the object of the devotion. Thus husbands grow to look like their wives, and sometimes *vice versa.* This is in direct contradiction to the more alarming theory held by Æ. Everyone knows that. But why are long-nosed men found in all the enclosures where the Cult of the Horse is being celebrated?

You meet them at the Spring Show, the Horse Show, Punchestown, Leopardstown, The Park, the Curragh, Fairyhouse and Baldoyle. Owners do not have it. That I will admit; but, then, owners as a rule take up owning horses late in life, when they have made their pile and, wishing to become fashionable and to rub shoulders with the best people, are converted to the Cult, just as anyone wishing to avoid poverty becomes a Christian Scientist. It is among the lifelong devotees the long nose is found. You might think that this comes from poking into race-cards; but you would be wrong. These men need no race-cards. They carry them only for the same reason that a priest carries his breviary, although he knows the words by heart. Among the 'stewards' are to be found the longest noses. They are of the inner sanctuary, as it were. Do not go away with the impression that I may give thought to a problem and find myself unable to solve it. I have the backing of science behind me in my solution. According to Darwin, the tapir was the prototype of the horse. Immemorial ancestry! The Cult goes back beyond recorded time.

With the women it is different. Their noses are not necessarily sharp. Leather pigskin has affected them. They have been so much in the saddle that the leather has entered into their soul. They wear country-looking tweeds, made far away from the country by London tailors, and low-heeled shoes. They walk as much like a horse walks round the paddock as they can; and when they can indulge their whim, they have stables in which they breed horses.

One of them, a Marchioness, caught sight of me. She was a very successful race-goer. She never had any losses. Hence the interest she was taking in my hospitable friend. He had warned me weeks earlier that if I met her to keep off a certain subject which was her besetting theme.

She stood with legs akimbo in front of me, a bulk of womanhood. Her voice was gentle. She really was a gentle lady when not crossed.

'What have you been doing with yourself?' she said.

'Lying fallow more or less.'

'See you again,' she smiled and moved on.

Her nose was blunt like the nose of a horse; and, like a horse, the sides of her face were flat. Why, then, when a horse has a blunt nose, should the noses of its votaries be long? Having strictly meditated this, I recognised the fact that those who had the longest noses spent all the Winter hunting the fox, and therefore there was a time element in the development of a nose. Owners, as I said, who, as a rule, are later postulants, have not had time to develop this 'proscenium of the face'.

Boss Croker, the owner of Orby, a Derby winner, had a stout nose like a pugilist. He was the only man with whom the King did not shake hands when he led in his winning horse. He had bid against His Majesty's representative at a sale of yearlings. He raised on his Glencairn estate the only Derby winner to be trained in Ireland.

Joe Magrath, the strong-armed man who saved his country when its fate was touch and go, is a great owner—he has a winner at nearly every meeting, yet he has a round nose.

The bookies were on their stands, shouting like muezzins. Refreshments were shut off until the end of the race. Ted's rumble seat was down. Bookies from the North were in evidence: Hughie McAlinden with the euphonious name was calling from his pinnacle. A fat English bookie laid the odds in guttural tones.

It may be very democratic to rub shoulders with every other worshipper; but I hate to be jostled. I hate to be butted in on when talking to a friend. I had this unpleasant experience at the rails in front of the Grand Stand. I had come across the Marchioness again, and she was asking me, 'not as a medical man but as an observant, intelligent human being', how I accounted for the fine fettle of the horse. I was wary at first, for this might be the very question of which I had been warned. Surely she is not going to give me Gulliver's Travels with its houyhnhnms with their neighing names? I was thinking of some non-committal answer, though the commitment in any case was not much, when up rushes a fellow with a small head and a jockey's ingrown chest and seized her programme. With a pencil he marked a paper.

'Thanks, Violet.'

He was about to rush away when I asked, 'Are you by any chance a stockbroker?'

He tried to look through me. I smiled blandly as I looked him up and down.

'Are you a stockbroker by any chance?' I repeated.

'What's that got to do with you?' he asked.

'I noticed that you have the manners of one. One glance at the market and off you go.'

Off he did go.

'You shouldn't have said that,' the Marchioness said. 'He fell off a horse and got concussion of the brain. Then he became a stockbroker; and a very successful one.'

'He owes his fortune to that concussion. His trade does not encourage imagination,' I concurred.

From the throats of tens of thousands of people came the dull cry, 'They're off!'

The shining horses passed us once. I watched the impassive faces of the monkey men who crouched on the horses' withers: watchful, alert, although their faces, with a deep line on either cheek, registered nothing.

Again they passed. This time they were in the straight, a cloud of colour with flashing limbs beneath. The turf became so sonorous as a drum. At last cheers broke the tension.

The board that announced the winners spelt out—Good Lord, it cannot be—SHANKS. If it spells out PAT I will consult an astrologer. But the final notice gave SHANKS MARE as the winner.

'So I thought,' the Marchioness remarked. 'What about some plovers' eggs?'

She led the way to the marquee of a Dublin club that found that exclusiveness was as bad an investment as the Exclusive, so it opened its doors to ladies in the last ten years. The air within was dank and hot and the grass underfoot greasy.

'I think we'll go to Ted's car.'

We left the enclosure and went to where the cars were parked. We found Ted's man dispensing lunch. When the Marchioness appeared the guests faded away.

James gave us seats in the sedan. He spread napkins on our knees.

As she sipped her champagne the Marchioness said, 'I asked you a question when poor Ned came to consult my card—for it is against his principles to buy one of his own—it is this: how do you account for the fitness, strength and speed of the horse?'

From the unnecessary look of rapture on her face I said to myself. 'It's coming now,' but I answered, 'Selective breeding.'

'Ah no,' she said. 'It's more than that.'

I remained silent but attentive.

'Can't you guess?'

Sadly I confessed, 'No.'

'Breast-feeding! Breast-feeding and nothing else.'

I saw four teats and only one foal.

'There's a lot in that,' I agreed.

'I should think there is. Take the case of yourself. I don't want to be personal—take the case of myself too. I can tell by you that you were a breast-fed baby. I—well, I will say this, I am not exactly a runt.'

She stretched her shoulders. ' The only child of mine that was not suckled because I got malaria is a disgrace to the family. He chases every woman he sees. He can't help it. He was deprived as an infant. . . . Now. . . .'

A man in pink, with a white face and white moustache under a tall hat, put his head through the window.

' So that's where you are. Violet, come out of it. You must watch the second race. People expect it.'

' Very well, Terence, I'll get going.' She lifted her bulk out of the car. ' You can stay here until Ted comes in or bore yourself stiff watching my mare lose.'

One of the aspects of Demeter was that of a mare. Under the appearance of the Mare-Headed she was worshipped in Arcadia, and may she not have appeared in this Western Arcadia to us?

Back in the enclosure people were lifting their hats. The new Prime Minister was driving in. No one pretended to be pre-occupied. They all looked at the Prime Minister's car with respect. Already he had done more in three months than his predecessor did in fifteen years. He didn't stall and wrap himself in a cloud of words. He did what his predecessor, for all self-exhortation, had failed to do—establish a Republic. Costello did more: he persuaded the Prime Ministers of the Dominions to accept his decision to sever political ties with England. This was done without ostentation or hesitation. The quiet dignity of the man made him popular when he went to Canada and convinced everyone of the justice of his determination. Not that politics is of such importance now that economics has supplanted it.

He finds time to visit the races.

Was there ever an Irishman who had not a sentiment for a horse? I remember convincing the late Pat Hogan, Minister for Agriculture, that not only had Disraeli done more for Great Britain than the ex-Prime Minister had done for Ireland; but he had attended the Derby; and that made him more English than his counterpart here was Irish. Pat agreed.

Loud cheers came from the fields outside. Who was coming now? Rumour that is never wrong at an open-air assembly said that Joe was coming. He had been detained on business at the Curragh, but he was in time for the third race.

The sea of heads bobbed before me. Sadly I thought: A few years, and they all shall have disappeared like clouds that cross a hill. Other generations shall take their place. How few of those present shall be missed? How few even remembered? Three or four; and one of these shall be

Joe Magrath, who has as many aspects as the Mare-headed One herself. Another will be William Cosgrove, who, in spite of his retiring disposition, will stand out for inflexible justice and honesty. And the present Prime Minister, Costello: he shall be remembered, not because he is in a series that is historical, but for the quality of his statesmanship; and for the fact that he is the first Republican Prime Minister.

Yet, in spite of this, and in spite of all his patriotism, his Government shall grow less and less popular because the Irish people outrun their Government every ten years (only the war saved the last Government). Like the Earth or the Marchioness, Ireland is a Mare-headed goddess. But, like Earth, she is also a goddess of death, and will enfold all her children in the end.

> 'It was Aed's, it was Ailill's,
> It was Conaing's, it was Cuiline's;
> The fort remains after each man in his turn—
> And the kings asleep in the ground.'

This is a foregone conclusion; but how would it be if in the crowded fields out there another Zozimus should arise under the rim of gentle hills, or another Blind Raftery who should seize the sentiment of all race-courses, of all Ireland, and give it to us in everlasting rhyme?

There is room for every kind of character in Ireland and no one is likelier to become popular than the man who is poor. There is some sort of luxury in pity, and when a man is pitiably poor all the more eligible is he for Tir na nOge.

The fact is that no Irishman can endure being himself for long. This is not only an Irish trait; but one that is universal. It is common alike to fool and sage. George Santayana, the wisest man of our time, has expressed this sentiment in a poem where he wishes to escape from himself. You don't have to be a hero to be a receptacle into which the Irish people precipitate themselves. Anyone will do—almost. But think of what Ireland will do to you once you become the receptacle of its spirit. Think of what happened to Parnell. Knowing this, no Irishman wants to be himself. He wants to be represented by a hero who, like the victim kings of primitive times, perished after a little reign.

I may be given to apprehensions which are groundless for the most part; but it is beginning to dawn on me that if I don't withdraw from the scene, I may become a national hero. Don't think I am getting a swollen head, it's not much of a compliment and so not much of a boast. Just look at the heroes we have had! After all, very few people know me. That's what makes me so eligible. And once you become a trash can for the soul of Ireland, the Marchioness, the Mare-headed, will get you surely. I have no wish to become a national hero; I had rather they threw bricks at me than themselves; but strong misgivings obsess me that I may be, if I do not get away. It will not be so fateful if I become a figure of edification far away.

CHAPTER TWENTY

Once Only

MAYBE ONCE a year, maybe not once in two or three years, the dream or vision comes to me of a small boy, who was myself, lying on the heather beside a mountain rivulet gazing down at a trout balanced about an inch or two above the sandy bottom of a little pool. Though the vision is pleasing, I do not linger on it because, though I am given to sentiment, I am not prone to being sentimental about myself.

Of late the vision has become more frequent, and so more insistent, for it recurs not only every week, but is before me night and day after every distraction or absorbing interest. The picture re-forms clearly and becomes clearer and clearer as the days return. This fact alone has made me decide to visit Roundwood and try to find again that mountain pool which cannot have been far from the house where I stayed; for a tiny boy may not wander far without being missed and chided on his return, and chided I was not.

To Roundwood, then, I resolved to go, prepared for the disappointment and the disillusion that is in store for all who seek to recapture the wonder and enthusiasm of their childhood. Beyond such a chasm as the years had deepened, what hope could I cherish to catch again the freshness and the magic that wood and rock and stream and hill held for a child who had been taken for the first time on a holiday from his native town?

I see that trout now as he lies safe below three feet of water, staying himself with an almost imperceptible movement of his transparent fins. I remember how I uncoiled a cast and tried to sink a fly that would not be submerged until I had tied a pebble to the gut and tried again. Down the fly went, and I held it in front of the little trout, but the trout took no notice of the lure. I returned to the house disappointed; but no one learned of my failure, for I was loath to acknowledge my inexperience, and I was far from certain that I had acted wisely in departing so drastically, through impatience, from the usual practice of anglers who wait for the fish to rise.

All I can remember that would mark the date is that it was a year of a great drought. The fish in the Vartry Lake were leaping two and three feet out of the water, and so close to the shore that I wondered why no one thought of putting a landing-net under them before they fell back. I see again distinctly (perhaps too distinctly, for memory is a magician) the crimson freckles above the band of gold which was their side, the brown of their backs that deepened into limpid black on the hard helmet of their heads; and I feel again the surprise and excitement of the suddenness with which they left the water, and the lovely curve of their leap into the air.

My trout lay so still near the bottom that I am beginning to wonder now if it were not a gudgeon, after all. Its back was greyish silver, and it was scarcely five inches long.

I remember the yellow-hammer that chirped incessantly, flashing black and yellow from its dipping tail as it swayed in the hedge between the road and the lake; but it will hardly be a landmark now.

Half a hundred years ago! Where will Beda Murphy be by this; and the maids who served that little inn?

From the railway station at Bray the drive was long, for there were no taxis, owing to the restrictions on motor fuel. A landau or a Victoria—one of those carriages that stretched between their pairs of wheels like an inverted Cupid's bow—was surely the kind of vehicle that took me to Roundwood in the days gone by. It seemed appropriate now. That's why I hired it. I liked the looks of the driver, a rubicund fellow in his early forties.

The drive was tedious, for the horse had to be walked up the many hills that led to the Rocky Valley. We stopped at Pluck's. Pluck may not own it now, for taverns change hands even as the Fort of Rathangan. The driver threw a rug across his horse and followed me into the bar parlour. There was nobody about. A round mahogany table, a horse-hair sofa and a few prints gave a non-committal greeting to all and sundry. Outside a hen could be heard clucking. Sunlight slanted down into a narrow yard. After a long wait the driver obligingly went to search of an attendant. A girl appeared and disappeared. We were more or less intruders. It seemed that we had come in at the side instead of at the front door under the white porcelain letters of J. Pluck. We apologised for being there at all. This confused the barmaid or the skivvy, or whatever she was, into action.

'What d'yez want?' she inquired.

The hen made a commotion as the maid returned with the drinks.

'Don't go away,' I said. 'We'll want the same again.'

We left with the feeling that the management had conferred a favour by suffering our presence in the place at all. The barmaid took the relish out of the tardy drinks.

We emerged under the shadow of a 'decent'

church that suggested with soaring spire heights yet to be won. The Rocky Valley was before us, the road escarped by granite boulders upthrust between broken acres of golden gorse. A few summer cottages hid among the rocks to the right under the shelter of a hill. After a slow climb the high ground on the right fell away and revealed a wide valley with a hint of a stream. The driver, who had failed to draw me into conversation, not for the want of a vocabulary but for fear that he might make the unforgivable mistake of taking a native for an American, began to thaw under the delayed action of the depth-charges we had put down at John Pluck's. He levelled his whip and, pointing to a large mansion of light brown stone crowned by a dome of green bronze, hardly visible in its trees, said:

'That's Powerscourt over there.'

'Powerscourt?'

'Yes, where the Battle of Agincourt was fought.'

On my answer depended his confidence.

'It seems to me that I heard something about movie men and a battle they staged here in Wicklow. So that is the place?'

'Begob, sir, you should have seen it. It took months. The longest battle I ever heard tell of. There was horses and spears and tents and knights in armour. You never seen the like.'

'Who ran it?' I asked and foolishly stopped the tide.

He had to consider what to him was a quite irrelevant detail. After much thought he said in a voice that had lost its enthusiasm: 'I think it was a man by the name of Rank was behind it.'

'Soldiers rank on rank,' I said, and was sorry for myself. It blows nobody good to gulp a drink. But the driver resumed the saga.

'They hired the Waterfall and pitched tents and bought up every old nag they could lay hands on and paid the boys well to dress up in armour and go charging at one another hell for leather with a long pole in their hand.'

'A pole?'

'Well, a spear. There's plenty of them about for keepsakes since. They have a round thing near one end and a point on the other. Regular spears they were, like the lancers used to have, only they had no flag on them. They spent a lot of money while they were at it. The "Powerscourt Arms" was full every night, and "The Royal" and every pub in Enniskerry. But they had to be up and mounted and ready to charge at cock-crow. And they kept the crowds out. That's why I'm thinking that they took Powerscourt because it has a wall about it to keep out the crowds.'

'But what had Lord Powerscourt to say to all this?'

'Sure wasn't it him that rented the demesne to

them? It was Her Ladyship that did any objecting there was.'

'Why should she object when His Lordship didn't?'

'There I leave you. Women is queer. They say that when she came across an arm, a leg or a nose that had been lopped off the day before, she would pick it up on her spiked stick and say, "What shall I do with this beastly thing?"'

The picture of Lady Powerscourt going the rounds like a park ranger collecting paper amused me. It must have been a great battle:

> 'Arms were from shoulders sent;
> Scalps to the teeth were rent.'

But I had to comment aloud on the tale he was telling me.

'It must have been shocking right enough to find a leg or a nose in the demesne.'

'Shure, they were only artificial legs that was lost the day before and never missed.'

'The casualties must have been heavy?' I suggested.

'Faith, you're right; but they were mostly French. The English won every day and the people didn't like it. They began to blame the management.'

'What could they expect? Wasn't it an English company that was running Agincourt in Powerscourt?'

He thought that out, and reluctantly agreed that what they were staging had the backing of history.

'But that's the way it happened in the old days. The French got the hell of a beating. It must be true, for a nephew of mine who worked in the battle for a month on the French side—and didn't like it—got such a belting that he turned on the Englishman, a fellow be the name of Houlihan, and he sez to him, "Houlihan," sez he, "Houlihan, get this into your head and under your helmet, and don't forget it: if ye larrup me on the last night the way ye have been doing up to this, be Jabers, I'll reverse history." It's history all right. That's how I know.'

I felt the need of silence to think this out. The great Sugar-Loaf was behind us now. The old Gaelic inhabitants called that and the lesser Sugar-Loaf the Silver Spears. In that lies history, too, and more than history. The Anglo-Saxons, lovers of creature comforts, thought of food. The more unsettled warrior Gaels thought of forays. Wicklow was a battle ground long before they staged Agincourt beneath the Sugar-Loaf.

The road was more level now and the horse was relieved from strain. I had not spoken since I heard that threat of the driver's nephew to 'reverse history'. When I thought of it, I realised that it was not as absurd as it sounded. For what have the movies been doing but reversing history, aye, and distorting it? In after years scholars will try to delve behind the only history that they shall have—movie history. But who will believe them?

The driver was talking to his horse. I accepted the cue and inquired after the horse's welfare. This started the driver into more history; but this time it was personal and contemporary.

'You think that the country is prosperous, but God forgive you! Do you know that if it wasn't for the Old Age pension the mare and I wouldn't have a bite to eat.'

Evidently it was my destiny to be astonished.

I had never seen the country looking more prosperous. The people appeared to be cheerful and well-fed: misery was nowhere to be seen. But now I am told that it is all as deceptive as a movie. And what am I to think of an Old Age pension for a man who cannot be near fifty yet, not to mention sixty-five? I was dumbfounded. At last I said:

'Do you tell me that you are in receipt of an Old Age pension?'

'Aye; and only for it I might as well retire.'

'But I thought'. . . . Where does thought lead me? I asked myself. The less I think the better. I began again:

'Surely there is an Inspector to interview you before the Government hands out an Old Age pension?'

'Av course there is; and two of them. But it was not me he seen at all; but an auld alibi out of the mountains.'

He jerked his whip over his left shoulder and indicated the O'Byrne County with its fastnesses and deep glens.

Again I was silenced. I pictured to myself that 'auld alibi', that old man of the mountains' suddenly finding himself of growing importance as the value of the Old Age pension dawned on the tribesmen of hill and glen. Just as he had settled down, determined 'to husband out life's taper at the close', he is thrust forward to represent his constituency, the younger generation, who are helpless when it comes to being suddenly matured enough to be pensionable. I longed to cast eyes on that 'auld alibi'. Maybe, I shall mcct him before my excursion ends. I have hopes, for I remembered Mahaffy's dictum, 'In Ireland the Inevitable never happens, the Unexpected always.'

After two hours the road passed by an artificial lake in fields to the left. Soon it afforded a glimpse of a natural lake, and then passed between three or four houses on either side. Two of the houses were longer and better kept than the others. They faced each other across the road. The house on the right was my destination.

The driver took my bag into the hall. He was

enjoying such a welcome that I wondered if there would be any left for me.

But I was mistaken. Instead of being left standing in the hall, I was taken into the kitchen, which is the principal room of a country house; but nowadays not open to strangers. To be admitted to the penetralia was a compliment I appreciated, for I knew what it meant.

The driver was well known to the owners. He was a mountainy man, a clansman who never drove past the house with a fare who might be a good customer. But now it was the driver who had to listen to local histories. A grave and ancient man was the speaker. The daughter of the old man was the woman of the house. She appeared to be a widow, for to a husband she did not refer. This by itself would be a poor proof of widowhood in a court of law, but we were in a home now and it had more import. After talking to me for a quarter of an hour she turned to the old man and, to his surprise, announced that I knew as much about the place as herself. I had been here as a boy. This took the conversation far into the night. It was late when I went along the corridor to my room. In the morning after breakfast I would begin to explore.

Through a thin screen of pines the Vartry Lake gleamed grey. That was over the road; but, as far as I remembered, it was on the hither side the little stream flowed down. I went through the garden at the back. A few apple-trees stood with arms akimbo, covered with silver moss. Through the fence I passed and walked to the right through the fields. There was no sign of a brook. That was strange. Mortal things pass away, but a running brook flows on. If I go back and out on the road and then turn into the fields or, better still, go on until I come to a bridge, I may find it. There was no bridge. Perhaps the stream was too small to need a bridge that would cause a rise in the road. I left the road and made a wide semi-circle high up in the fields, but no brook was there. Then I thought of the heather. Maybe it was from a picnic I had stumbled upon the brook. The heather began far away, so far away I went. The ground rose brokenly into what in Scotland they call 'braes'. A high bank, too high to see what was above it without a climb, rose before me. What is that? Distinctly I heard the sound of water falling hidden from the eye. I should have known that in such broken ground the rivulet would be hidden. I reached the bank. I saw the little pool, with a wall of rock rising upright beyond it covered with brown wet moss. A broken trickle of water fell down to fill the pool. Eagerly I took in every detail: heather, ferns, moss, a leafy branch spreading half across to hide the pool from above. Would I look for the trout and risk a disappointment, or be satisfied with what I had found?

It was not any wonder that I had failed to find it at once. It lay low in the heather under a wall of wet rock, covered with dark brown moss, a few ferns and branches from a willow that took root out of sight. It was just a little basin in a mountain stream. But how clear it was! Had it not been for the ripple where the water fell into it, I could not have been sure where its surface ended and the air began. It was as crystal as the eyes of a wondering child.

I tried to see it as I had seen it for the first time. The branches I did not remember; but everything else was there: the trickle from the rock, the tinkle behind me where the overflow hid in the heather again, and the granite dust that formed its sandy floor. There was another difference: I could reach down an arm and touch the floor that had seemed so out of reach.

It was exhilarating, this sense of accomplishing something by my discovery. I realised now that it was not all a dream and that the persistent vision had its origin in reality. I stood up to follow with my eyes the course of the stream to where it went under the road. Just as I thought: it had not a bridge to itself. Instead, it passed through a square tunnel of cement, walled above the road like the side of a bridge. I marked the place. It was not more than a few furlongs from the inn. Hedges started again, gapped where the walls were. I could not miss it even in the dark.

How long I lay beside my pool I do not know. The morning was still young. Half an hour would take me home when I wished to go.

I rose. I did not gaze down to see if there was a fish in that little pool. Instead, I leapt across it and caught hold of the boskage beside the tiny waterfall. I climbed up the rock and worked my way along the narrow channel of the stream. I have loved streams all my life, and I enjoyed wading up against the brook and splashing from half-hidden pool to pool. The climb grew steeper. I scaled many a replica of the pool I had left far below. I passed between two boulders on the level ground where the stream was absorbed amongst mosses and ferns. The ground grew firm and dry. I turned around the last bush of golden gorse that bloomed by the way, under a solitary boulder of granite, and a strange sight met my astonished eyes.

I had come upon a town not two hundred yards away. Houses and streets, carriages and horses, men and women and children, and the cheerful hum of life. A church beside its tall steeple that held a clock with gilt hands on a black dial. The church was the only building out of proportion. Another ' picture ' in the process of being ' shot ', I guessed. But there were no guards or fences to turn me back. I walked along the first street I came to, and looked about me. Shops and offices and private houses lined the way. Smoke rose from the chimneys, for the weather, though bright, can be cold in Ireland even in the summer. Motor-cars and motor-bicycles were absent. It was as if you were in Bermuda or some town in old Japan. A period picture, evidently. And yet there was no apparent sign that the buildings had been thrown up temporarily. They looked far more solid and substantial than anything I had seen in the studios of the West Coast. Whatever company is financing this must intend the set to be permanent for period plays.

Every detail has been carefully studied. The houses show signs of weathering. Even the cast-iron railings that guard the areas of houses that evidently are intended to represent town houses of the eighteenth century are eroded where they join the stonework below. Plate glass is absent from any of the windows, which are lit by many panes. Even the pavement shows signs of wear. An old town seems to have been transplated completely; the trees that line the public squares are mature.

'Are you looking for anyone, mister?' a bare-footed street urchin inquired.

I shook my head; he doffed his cap and went away. He is better-mannered than many I have met in the course of my many wanderings.

Down the street came a two-seated trap or carriage with the horses in tandem. That was a sight I had not seen for years. The man who drove it wore a tall silk hat. Though a young man, he sported side whiskers. Beside him sat a 'tiger' or little groom. He raised his whip in salute as he passed. I turned to see if there were anyone beside me for whom it was intended, for I could not take it that he meant the salute for me. There was no one passing. Strange!

Two ladies approached. On one side walked a little boy. He wore a large collar outside his coat and he walked demurely with his toes turned out. When he saw me he seized one of the ladies' hands. His mother and his governess, whoever they were, wore clothes that seemed strange to me. Their skirts swept the pathway and their sleeves were puffed out like legs of mutton and rose over the shoulders in two peaks. Their boots were buttoned higher than the ankle, the same as those worn by the small boy. They carried umbrellas with long handles. They walked leisurely, talking the while without hurry or even purpose. It seemed as if they were out merely to take the air. The singular absence of crowds was the only sign that there was a limit to the number of the supers. Look wherever I would, no policeman appeared on point duty. I failed to find a policeman anywhere, or any sign of traffic lights. There was not a telephone wire in the town.

Down a street a two-horse bus or tram came gaily, with a copper bell jingling between the horses. It ran on iron tram-lines. These, too, were spread from wear and tear. I went down a street at right angles to the one by which I had entered. Crowds here were lining the way. A hum of excitement ran amongst them. A procession of some kind was about to pass. I took a place three steps up in front of one of the houses to get a better view. Presently a large coach came on, suspended by great leathern straps. Four horses drew it, driven by a fat and bewigged coachman with golden epaulets; beside him sat a footman similarly dressed. Within the coach, which had large windows of glass, sat an alderman with a lady beside him. On the seat in front of them lay a huge silver mace, on a dark velvet cushion.

The crowd cheered and waved handkerchiefs. The Lord Mayor. He bowed in acknowledgement of the cheers. Behind him, in gay red vests and helmets of shining brass, came the town's Fire Brigade. They drove by, riding in or clinging to fire engines, hose-carriers and a long ladder shining with fresh brown varnish. After these came what appeared to be the various guilds of the town, with large banners pictured with their emblems. Behind the banners walked men in civilian clothes, some of whom wore gold-fringed sashes across their breasts.

They marked time like soldiers, when the procession slowed at a turn. They marched gravely without turning to look at the cheering crowd. Suddenly a bucket of water or of some fluid fell on my head and the heads of those who were standing shoulder to shoulder by me. We looked up. A small boy was held dangling by one leg from a top window of the house on the steps of which we were standing. A man who was holding him leant out of the window and waved his free hand. We took his gesture for a sign that he was punishing the boy for his mischievous act. After a while the procession moved past, and I was left standing on the house steps alone. I took out a handkerchief and began to dry my hat and coat, when the door opened behind me, and a lady, who looked like one of those whom I had met out walking, appeared and said gently, 'Won't you come in?' She spoke with quiet dignity, yet I knew that she was disturbed.

I removed my hat and entered a large hall with a brass rail just inside the door. A deer-horn receptacle for umbrellas and walking-sticks was just inside it. At the back rose a tall grandfather clock. Chairs stood against the walls, and over a fireplace was a large picture framed in cane of a paddle-steamer gay with bunting passing a crowded pier with a lighthouse at one end.

'We are extremely sorry for what has happened.

My son, I am afraid, is very bold. Rest assured that he will be corrected.'

I made light of the incident, 'accident', I called it. I bowed and turned to go.

'You cannot go,' the lady said. 'You must have your wet clothes dried thoroughly, and you must stay to lunch. My husband will be in shortly, and will be glad to see you. He will not be pleased when he hears of Alec's escapade. He spoils the child.'

As she spoke a key turned in the latch and a small man in his early middle age entered the hall. He wore whiskers, like the rest of the cast. He looked at me in no unfriendly way, and then looked inquiringly at his wife.

'Alec threw a basin of water on the people who were standing on the steps of the hall door. This gentleman got the most of it. I have asked him to lunch while his coat is being dried.'

He extended his hand.

'If you have not noticed my name on the door—I don't suppose you did—it is Purefoy. I am a doctor. This is my wife.'

'It is extremely kind of you,' I said, 'but I cannot think of trespassing on your hospitality. After all, the accident was due to a boyish prank. I am wet already (I glanced at my shoes) through wading along a mountain stream.'

He followed my gaze, but apparently he saw nothing odd about my shoes. After a pause.

'Nevertheless,' he said, 'lunch is just ready.' He looked at his watch as if to confirm his statement. 'We will not let you go. Thackeray will attend to you. . . . Oh, Thackeray,' as the butler appeared, 'while this gentleman's coat is being dried, I will give him one of mine.' He led me upstairs and, turning to his wife, said, 'We won't be very long. Better tell Miss Orr.'

We entered a large room made smaller by a double bed and mahogany wardrobes with three doors. He went to one and selected a dark coat for me. I handed my own coat to the butler, and I put the jacket on.

Dr. Purefoy smiled and said:

'It's as near a fit as these things go.'

He took me by the arm, and in that friendly fashion we went down to lunch.

We entered another large room furnished with heavy mahogany chairs, sideboard and dumb waiters. Silver shone on the sideboard. On a dark grey marble mantelpiece in front of a mirror that went up to the ceiling stood a bronze clock between two bronze urns. From the direction of one of the windows Mrs. Purefoy advanced, and with her another lady who was obviously the governess, Miss Orr. I recognised them both now. I had seen them in the street.

Dr. Purefoy still guiding me by the arm led me forward and said, 'I think he should have a hot drink with his lunch.'

If these people are rehearsing, I thought, it must be the most thorough rehearsal to which any cast was ever subjected. Every word, every detail is Victorian. Was there ever such a scrupulous training for any play? I thought of the thoroughness and passion for detail that made Austin Strong have his eyes bandaged for three months in order to realise the problems that confront the blind. That was one man in a million; but here everybody was subjected to a discipline that must be exacting in the extreme. Even in their friendliness there was such a genteel reserve that I forbore—for I dared not be rude enough—to ask directly what they were playing at. I preferred to fall in with the play.

Miss Orr was gently bantered on the misconduct of her charge. She turned the rallery gracefully.

'All's well that ends well, we must admit.' Shyly she glanced at me.

'Yes, Alec has brought us pleasant company,' Mrs. Purefoy conceded.

'Through no fault of his own,' the doctor said.

'I would have invited the baptism had I known its advantages,' I replied, trying to return the very polite compliment of Miss Orr.

To my surprise that young lady blushed.

After the fish, the butler placed a large cover dish on the table in front of the doctor, removed the lid with a little flourish and revealed a leg of lamb. This the doctor proceeded to carve. The butler handed round each plate as it was filled. 'Well, if this is not carrying the thing far, I'll be' . . . I said, but I said it to myself. I felt disinclined even to think otiosely in that company. I begged to be excused from drinking whisky punch so early.

Claret in coloured wine-glasses was served with the lunch. Neither of the ladies drank wine.

The talk was of the opera and of the fullness of the house. They were going to hear Madame Patti sing.

I asked Miss Orr if she liked grand opera. She said that she did, but that she preferred Chamber music. She seemed embarrassed to talk before the doctor and his wife.

The thought struck me—her employers were not including her in their party. A bread-pudding filled with raisins was next dispensed. Cream in a large silver ewer was passed round. I handed mine first to Miss Orr. She poured a little of the cream daintily on the pudding and passed the ewer to me.

The doctor rose and apologised for leaving before the end of lunch.

'But you will understand,' he said to me.

That was the only inkling, if it were so intended,

that I got of his being wanted on the set. I supposed that they were glad to have me to test themselves out, as it were. I dismissed the thought, for it was uncomplimentary even to myself. Yet when we went upstairs to the drawing-room the idea recurred. They were rehearsing a Victorian 'at home'. I was the foil, the visitor.

The drawing-room was the largest room in the house. It went across the width of the building, and was lit by three windows giving on the street. There were three large mirrors: two with the console tables and one over the mantel, as in the room below. One console table was very large. It covered half the side-wall of the room. In the centre stood a strange article of furniture. It was a piece that was comprised of four seats back to back. The middle of the sofa or divan was crowned with an urn carved from walnut. A grand piano took up one corner. Gilt clocks under glass domes with porcelain dials painted with Watteau-like scenes stood on the console tables. Here and there tables with glass tops showing bric-à-brac took up most of the space that remained. On the mantelpiece two lustre candelabra with long crystal pendants ornamented that marble shelf.

The ladies seated themselves on satin-covered chairs. I stood behind a chair the back of which was covered by a mother-of-pearl inlay, until I was invited to be seated. I felt very conscious of my rough costume and my wet shoes, which their politeness forbade them to notice.

'I am sorry that my husband had to go out. I never know when he may be called. You know the way it is.'

I nodded my head.

'Do you never accompany him?'

'Oh come, come.'

'You both are very photogenic,' I ventured.

They would not depart one iota from character. I knew that before they pretended not to know what I meant.

'You photograph well,' I said again.

They turned to one another.

'Evangeline, bring down the photographs.'

Miss Orr left the room.

'It is impossible to get Alexander to sit still. Mr. Lawrence has to fix his head with an iron bracket before he takes his photograph. Miss Orr will show you what I mean.'

Miss Orr returned and gave a set of photographs in tissue paper directly into my hands. What is more, she stood behind me and leant over my shoulder as I unwrapped them.

I saw a small boy with a lace collar and large 'sailor' hat standing on a rustic bridge. In his left hand he held a fishing-net, the handle of which obviously served to steady him on the bridge. His full, broad face was turned to the beholder. Long golden ringlets fell down to his neck.

So that's the brat who inundated me, I thought, as I summoned a look of interest to my face. I turned to a second photograph. The subject was the same. I knew that if I turned my face it might touch the face of Miss Orr, who was leaning over my shoulder. I shuffled the pack of photographs.

'Does he like fishing?' I asked the governess.

It sounded very flat; but it was all I could say at the moment. To comment upon the likeness of a boy I had hardly seen would, I felt, be bad form. I pretended an interest I was far from feeling:

'Are there any more?'

'Oh, yes,' said Mrs. Purefoy, rising and going to an escretoire, from which she took half a dozen cases bound in black morocco. One she opened by pressing a spring. A daguerreotype in a pinchbeck frame of an old lady in a silk dress which made her look like a house-keeper met my eye.

Miss Orr's face left my shoulder.

'My poor dear mother!' Mrs. Purefoy said.

'Miss Lacey is here now, Madam,' Thackeray announced.

That, being interpreted, meant that Miss Lacey was not a visitor, but some sewing-maid. This proved to be the right interpretation.

Mrs. Purefoy excused herself, explaining that she had to try on her opera dress. I was about to go when she added:

'I will leave you two alone for a little while. You cannot go until your coat is dry.'

Miss Orr stood behind me. I turned half around when Mrs. Purefoy had gone through the door which Thackeray held open. I looked her in the eyes.

'When do you go on?' I asked, summoning my courage.

The result of my question was surprising. Miss Orr went over and sat on one of the four joined seats in the middle of the room. She bent her head into her hands. Her shoulders shook.

'Take me out of this,' she moaned. 'Oh, take me away.'

I wondered what book they were screening and what was her part. Something that had to do with an elopement, evidently. But why all this waste of energy. There was no one to see her.

Tears fell through her fingers; sobs shook her.

Good heavens! can she be in earnest? I asked myself.

'Why do you want to get away?' I asked. 'You know that I am old enough to be your father.'

She looked up with eyes like violets drenched and said:

'You are not half as old as that awful man.'

'The doctor?'

She nodded.

'But you have Mrs. Purefoy to protect you?' I said.

'She's worse.'

I saw the position in a flash, a pandering wife.

'Take me away,' she said again.

'But . . . how? How could you leave this?' I asked. 'When do you mean to go?'

'Any time. Any time. To-night when they are at the opera.'

She rose from her seat and fell on my neck. If there were ever an embarrassing position I was in one. Two heavy plaits contained her hair. I noticed that it curled in a golden ringlet behind her ear, and that it had seemed dark brown to me, which goes to show how much my mind must have been in abeyance that I should notice in a crisis such a trivial thing.

'Promise to take me away.'

'What is preventing you from going? Can't you ask for another character?'

'She will not give me one. Oh, promise, promise me.'

I was about to ask, 'What will I do with you?'

when I remembered that only a fellow like George Moore would do a thing like that. The code they taught me lays it down that you do not argue with a woman who invites you to elope. She has given herself away. Do not make it harder for her. Go thou, etc.

'Where can we meet?' was all I said.

'By the church at eight. It will be dusk by then. There will be a service to-night. No one will notice me.'

I confess that, code or no code, it did seem strange the way she recovered her wits. Mine were still dispersed. While I was trying to gather them :

'Promise,' she implored.

I could feel how round her arms were in their black silk sleeves of her governess's dress, her badge of servitude. All at once the pathos of her position overwhelmed me. I promised. She released me and walked slowly to a window. It was just in time, for Thackeray appeared with :

'Your coat is ready, sir.'

When I came back to the drawing-room, the ladies were preparing tea. Very politely I refused to join them. Where was it I had heard that on your first visit to lunch in a strange house it is not done to remain on to tea? The clock in the church steeple chimed five. I looked at my watch. It marked four o'clock. They had never heard of Summer time, I realised.

'You must come again,' Mrs. Purefoy said.

'I should love to.'

As I said it, I wondered if I would be welcomed again.

Outside I decided to have a look at the town. First of all I must locate the church I had seen when I first found the place. It stood past some flowering-trees at the top of a slight incline. It was not very far from the house I had just left. Round a corner, I retraced my steps and saw it. The black dial with the gilt hands pointed to a quarter past five. My watch was one hour slow. I had ample time to see the town. I was curious to find out for myself how far the thoroughness of the set-up went. The few shops I visited had shopkeepers who were familiar with their stock-in-trade. In one, a wine merchant's, I was invited into a back parlour by an old gentleman with charming manners. He would be what an old-fashioned lady would call 'a superior person'. Nowadays we would wonder how he escaped an O.B.E.

His lore was the outcome of the experience and study of a lifetime. He lit a gas-lamp and began to explain that wine was a living thing and that it had to be humoured as much as a wayward child (I thought of Alec and of all he had let me in for), port particularly, he said.

His ledgers were all kept in longhand. As he turned the pages over he spoke of many titled clients whom it was his privilege to supply. I felt that it was they who were privileged when he helped me to a second glass of port.

'You must forgive me from sampling a different pipe. As you grow older your palate will mature.'

Then the explanation of the whole thing came to me. The promoters, whoever they are, have decided to emulate by reconstruction a town that will provide all the ease and comfort of a departed age to people whom the helter-skelter 'the sick hurry and divided aims' of our time have distracted and driven half insane.

Rockefeller restored Williamstown; but here they have gone farther: they have restored the period and the peace that enfolded its deliberate and sedate life of tangible joys. Old world it is; but, oh, the freshness of it all! A great idea, I thought, to go back fifty or a hundred years and build a model slumless town that would be a refuge from this runagate delirium of to-day.

As I left the house of the wine merchant, I looked back. I would call again. The brass plate on the door of his Georgian house read:

SIR GEORGE BRENT

A shining brass knocker. A brass-bound orifice

marked ' Letters '. No more. That was an admirable touch! So they knighted good wine merchants instead of cirrhotic ex-Indian Civil Servants in those days.

It was getting on to six o'clock. Already boys were carrying one by one shutters, which they fitted to the windows from the outside. It would take time to make arrangements for the accommodation of Evangeline. It would not be necessary to explain the circumstances. I could send her to Dublin next day. I did not think that there would be a hue and cry before that. It would not be until she failed to appear at breakfast that her absence would be noticed.

Miss Murphy was delighted, she was sure. There were many empty rooms. All that she had to do was to ' air ' one of them. Would the lady be coming to dinner? I thought not. They were dining early, so as to go to the opera. So that was the way it was. This I confirmed. Would they send the trap for her? I thought that it would not be required. I said, ' Leave that to me '.

It was six-thirty when I set out to keep my promise. I gave myself ample time, because I intended to enter the town from the same approach rather than take the risk of failing to find it. I would walk, keeping the stream in sight; so that, if I approached by any other entrance, especially after dusk, I should know it.

I walked rapidly, so as to reach the stream while the light lasted. Once I had that for a guide, I could take my time till darkness gathered.

This time I took the road and, leaping over a cement wall, followed the course of the brook. I would skirt the rock and wait by the pool until it began to grow dusk. In the town they were an hour before us, for we were on Summer time.

By half-past six I had reached the gorse-ringed rocks. I will shelter here for a quarter of an hour more. I will have time to reach the church and meet Evangeline. What was I letting myself in for? Was she quite sane? Maybe the doctor and his wife were sheltering her in their home and that she was subject to harmless hallucinations. For instance, what did she mean by saying that I was not half the doctor's age? If he were fifty, which I doubted, that would make me twenty-five. But hallucination or no, I had given my word to be at the church by eight. The light was fading now.

I turned round the rock and stared. There was no town! I walked forward to where I was sure a street had been, a street that started immediately out of gorse and heather as in a studio. There was neither street nor house. I looked back to get my bearings. There was no mistaking the rock. It was from that I went forward for a hundred yards, and here I am where the street with its comely houses on each side and, round the corner, the church with its clock tower, had been.

Maybe, maybe, in the light of day it was farther than I thought. I rushed forward until the heather was up to my waist and I began to stumble between the tussocks. What can have happened? They could not remove even a village circus in an hour. They could remove nothing without leaving scars on the grass. The town was gone, the town where I had walked on firm pavement, where I had spoken to the citizens and eaten and drunk with them. That town was no subjective thing.

I thought of Evangeline under the tower waiting in vain for me. Once more I asked myself could I be in the right place. Had I not made a mistake by skirting the stream instead of wading up against the current? But still the unmistakable gate, the rock, was there. No town!

I did not know what to do or to think. I doubted my sanity. What magical trick was here, 'not a wrack behind!' I had a profound distrust of substantial things.

Overhead, in the middle air, I heard the chime of a bell.

CHAPTER TWENTY-ONE

Green Tape

THE BRANCH OFFICE of the Munster and Leinster Bank was empty, not because of an economic war with England (that is another story) but because it was the lunch hour. I had come to see the manager; but he was at lunch. He would be back 'any minute now'. Delays were becoming a treat to me. Had I not already waited two months and seven days for a seat on a Transatlantic plane that was to take off 'any minute now'? That minute was approaching: it might be tomorrow. You never could tell. To judge by the advertisements, it was quicker to go to New York than to Cork, from actual experience of the train. So I lolled about the branch office, which was decorated by a calendar and a clock. The sound of an adding machine being tuned somewhere off carried the life of the bank over the lunch hour. Behind some vertical brass bars I thought I heard a sound of breathing. I crept close, taking the utmost precaution not to alarm whomever it might be. I stood still, hardly daring to respire.

I glanced at the clock. Its hands were together. It was ten past two. I moved so that I could see diagonally through the bars. A blond young man was leaning over a black box of japanned metal. Fascinated, I stared transfixed. My gaze must have aroused him. Without lifting his eyes from the contents of the box, he murmured, 'Any minute now'.

A sound behind me broke the tension. A hand must have moved from outside, for one half of the swing door was thrust open and a man entered with rapid strides and two raincoats. He was spare, with square shoulders and a broad, red face. He took one look round the bank. The adding machine opened up; its staccato speech filled the air with sound. The newcomer turned and eyed me. I felt that the youth behind the bars had suddenly risen to his feet. He was coming closer as the man with the raincoats approached. I was between the two, with the adding machine on my right under the screened window. Abruptly the man with the overcoats removed his hat, changed it to his left hand and, holding his right hand out in greeting, stood and said with a slow smile:

'The poetry of motion!'

It was McWilliam Lynch, the sprinter. He referred to our days on the track when I used to compete in cycling events and he did the hundred yards dash.

A voice behind me whispered in awestruck tones:

'That's the manager!'

The manager and I shook hands. He seized me by the elbow and, rushing me across the floor, led the way to an inner room which a quick glance at the flying door marked 'Manager' told me was his office. The door swung to behind us. The manager hung up his hat. He pointed to a chair with polished arms.

'It must be fifty years ago,' he said.

I was about to assent when he held up his hand in a gesture that indicated silence and conveyed a warning at the same time. He tip-toed to a large safe or strong room embedded in the wall, swung the combination and produced two glasses and a bottle of Tullamore Dew. He spun the bottle in his hand, making a movie of the label.

'Twenty years old,' he said. 'I wish I was twenty years old again. I would be doing better than around twelve for the hundred.'

'Metres,' I inquired.

'Not likely. The hundred yards dash. I did that the other day in the Veterans' race.'

'By heavens, you're not a day older. What age are you, anyway?'

He said nothing, but raised his eyes to a clock over my head on the wall behind me. He filled himself another shot. I thought it an opportune moment to ask his help.

'What can I do for you?' he asked.

'I have run out of cash; but I have a cheque book . . .'

'Fill it in! Fill it in! Any amount. You see that clock? I shall be retired in ten minutes. Fifty years of service! Fill it in!'

'I have run out only of English money. This is a dollar cheque-book.'

'And what's wrong with that? Fill it in, and hurry up.'

'Well, of all the banks I have ever come across, this one beats Banagher.'

He pressed a bell. The blond young man appeared.

"How do you want it?' the manager asked me. 'Small denominations? Cash that.'

The blond youth went out gazing at the cheque.

While he was gone we resumed our conversation. It was the manager's last day, last hour, in the Bank. He had bought a house on the river. He had all he wanted. He would make way for younger blood: give the boys a chance.

'When I came in and found the bank empty it put me in mind of the famous bank in the Midlands during the so-called economic war.'

'I know the bank. What did you hear?'

'I heard that there was no report from that branch for three weeks. None of the letters from

Headquarters was answered, so they sent an Inspector down. He arrived and, right enough, the bank was empty. He had not expected to see any customers; but he did expect to see the staff. There was no sign of any of them anywhere. He rapped on a door. No answer. He tried a second door. It was locked. He went behind the rails and tried another door. Locked. Behind the third door he thought he heard voices. He listened. After a while he heard someone say:

'"Have a heart? I pass."

'Indignantly he tried the handle, but the door was locked. He hammered on the panel.

'"Who's there?" a voice asked.

'"The Inspector."

'"Well, the gas meter's in the cellar."

'"But—but I'm the bank Inspector."

'Silence. Then a voice: "The books are on the shelf. Inspect away."

'He was speechless. At last his eye fell on the fire alarm. To teach the young pups a lesson, he pulled it. That would get them out. For a minute nothing happened. He looked out of the window, and in front of his eyes a pot-boy from the hotel across the street came hurrying with four pints of Guinness on a tray.'

McWilliam Lynch slapped his thigh. His eyes sparkled.

'That banks had liquid assets all right.'

The blond clerk came in with the change. When he had gone, McWilliam Lynch put the bottle and the glasses in the pockets of his raincoat.

'This bank has liquid assets *go leor* without this!' he remarked as we steered for the door.

It is a pity that I could not go that night to the dinner in honour of the retiring manager who had preserved his fitness for over fifty years. Seventy years young he was, and no mistake. Think of any man sprinting a hundred and beating men twenty years his junior at his time of life!

A man is all right in Ireland if he can keep time out of his joints.

Apart from its uncertainty, air travel restricts luggage, so I had to arrange to have my suitcases sent by sea. In order to do this an export licence must be obtained from the Government. But the Government office was in Dublin. To Dublin I had to go. Back to Limerick after, so as to be near the unaccountable plane. Forms had to be filled giving a list of socks, shirts, under- and over-wear, otherwise nothing may be exported from the country. To save weight my typewriter had to be sent by sea. Green tape was enveloping the tourist trade.

I had little difficulty in getting an export permit, because the Government is familiar with those whom smuggling interests, and I was not included among its familiars. There was far more trouble in getting my traps out of the control of the Customs.

The muddle of red tape is everywhere, and it thrives on its latest host, air travel. This curse of red tape is by no means confined to Ireland. It has grounded air lines and put thousands of travellers under what is tantamount to open arrest all over the world. I, as a sorry instance, could not risk taking an hour off from a vigil by the airport; and yet I had to come to Dublin to send my heavy stuff by sea. Two thousand years ago a man could travel from York to Byzantium with more dispatch and less annoyance than he can do now trammelled by passports, re-entry certificates, fingerprints, parents' marriage-lines and police releases.

I had to go to the quays for a shipping form. I was not permitted to fill it in without instructions. The shipping clerk had joined the great majority of those who would be back in a minute. After an hour, he returned or came in, for all I know it may have been his first visit to the office that morning. At last I gave from memory another list of what my suitcase contained. I had to take it to the customs shed—not Custom House any more. This was a mile off along the North Wall.

At the end of a shed a little fellow with an insignificant head was absorbed in another sheaf of 'forms'. He took no notice of me, although I was the only caller to the place. I knocked on the counter. At long last he came over reluctantly. When he read my name he became animated. He cried out in delighted surprise.

'Well, if this isn't a coincidence! My mother always said that I was the dead spit of you, and here you are!'

Though I am shy by nature and easily embarrassed, I accepted the compliment because my luggage was accepted with 'To hell with the list'.

Thank God, my fears of becoming a national hero are unfounded. We smiled our adieux.

Of one thing a traveller should be mindful when he revisits a country that seems to him to be changed: the change that is in himself must not be forgotten.

I must bear in mind that I am like a clerk in a clearing-house.

That which appears to be aged, torpid and outworn will to younger and more eager eyes be as fresh and bright as the Liffey in its high mountain cradle in Kippure. The old town has weathered many vicissitudes without my help; and I should be the last to attribute any more to her now. There will always be new and original characters in Dublin and, relying on that, I would not have the Liffey change its bed or cease from rolling down the lea.

THE END

ANNOUNCEMENT

The chapters of *Rolling Down the Lea* in which Dr. Gogarty describes his journey to Galway and to Connemara (Chapters X–XVI) have a remarkable and delightful counterpart in a long and hitherto unpublished letter written over one hundred years ago by

MARIA EDGEWORTH

to her youngest brother Pakenham Edgeworth in India. This letter gives a detailed and spirited account of a

TOUR IN CONNEMARA IN 1833

undertaken by Maria Edgeworth in company with a rich philanthropist and his wife. It displays to admirable advantage the humour, keen observation and gay acceptance of discomfort characteristic of Maria Edgeworth, who was sixty-six years of age at the time of her journey. She visited and portrays several of the places mentioned by Dr. Gogarty, and the contrast between the two so different travellers give piquancy to both their narratives.

TOUR IN CONNEMARA IN 1833
by MARIA EDGEWORTH

is edited by her great nephew, Harold Edgeworth Butler, and published in period-style as a foolscap octavo volume with a folding map. The edition is limited to five hundred copies.

CONSTABLE · LONDON

Printed in Great Britain by
RICHARD CLAY AND COMPANY, LTD.
B U N G A Y
SUFFOLK